Small Hotels of London

Sari Barbour & Caroline Squires

drawings by Jean-Pierre Moal

MPC

Published by:
Moorland Publishing Co Ltd,
Moor Farm Road West,
Ashbourne,
Derbyshire DE6 1HD
England

ISBN 0 86190 518 0

1st edition 1993
2nd revised edition 1994

British Library Cataloguing in Publication Data:
A catalogue record for this book is available from the British Library.

Printed in Great Britain by:
The Cromwell Press Ltd,
Broughton Gifford, Wilts

Contents

Key to Price Symbols

£   Up to £30 single and £45 double

££   £30-£45 single and £45-£60 double

£££ £45-£60 single room and £60-£75 double

££££ £60-£75 single room and £75-£90 double

Voucher Scheme

Each of the vouchers at the end of this book entitles the guest to a discount of £5 at hotels marked '£5 voucher scheme'. A few of the hotels have certain other requirements, such as a minimum stay of two nights. If so, this is made clear in the text. The voucher **must** be mentioned when making a reservation and is valid for 1994 and 1995. Only one voucher may be used per establishment.

Maps

The maps in this book on pages 11 and 95, show the location of the areas covered in this book, and enable the visitor to plan where to stay. Each entry has a brief description of how to find the hotel using public transport, but for greater detail use a street map of London, such as Geographer's A-Z, Geographia or Bartholemew. Maps are also obtainable from the London Tourist Board and London Transport.

About the Authors

Sari Barbour and Caroline Squires are both well equipped to write about their subject, having spent many years in the tourism business in London.

Both worked for the London Tourist Board, where they met and decided to write this book, having gained vast experience inspecting and reserving hotels and learning to match the traveller, whether on business or holiday, with the right accommodation for their needs.

They have worked in a number of small hotels in London over the years and have also at times provided bed and breakfast in their own homes.

Introduction

A Special Selection

Small Hotels of London is a very personal, and totally independent, selection of a wide range of medium-priced, individually inspected hotels. **None of them has paid, or been asked to pay**, for entry to this guide book.

The first edition of this book proved to be enormously popular and in this edition several new areas of London have been introduced as well as a number of delightful new hotels.

Each of these hotels has something special to offer the visitor: one, you will find, has spectacular views over the River Thames, another is right in the heart of Theatreland, and yet another will make you feel so cossetted that you will be disinclined ever to set foot outside the door!

A number are furnished with beautiful antiques and some (particularly in Outer London) have lovely gardens in which guests may relax at the end of the day, or perhaps join in a barbecue on a warm summer evening.

Some of the hotels in Bloomsbury are able to provide guests with access to private tennis courts; others in the Paddington area have free parking right in the centre of London and we even found a hotel which offers home-made bread, freshly baked each morning.

What to Expect

Variety and friendliness are the hallmarks of these hotels, quite different from the impersonal chain hotels which dominate our cities nowadays. Most are run by the proprietors themselves, whose standards are high and who really enjoy being with their guests and helping them find their way around the city.

Few of these small hotels are purpose-built, most being conversions of eighteenth- and nineteenth-century houses, constructed in the days when families had many children and as many servants. Anyone who has watched the TV series 'Upstairs Downstairs' will recognise this type of house, many of which retain their fine moulded ceilings, elegant staircases and original fireplaces.

Space is at a premium in London and, generally speaking, bedrooms are smaller here than in equivalent hotels in the USA, Australia etc. The facilities and services provided by the hotels are clearly detailed in the text. Many have now installed lifts (elevators) but there are still a number without, and rooms can be as high as the third or fourth floors (there is a special section for disabled on page 156). Similarly, some hotels have formal restaurants and bars, while others serve only breakfast. The provision of tea/coffee making facilities is becoming ever more widespread, as are hairdryers, and the more expensive hotels often have trouser-presses. Flower boxes are a feature of London hotels and you will find few whose façades are not brightened by colourful displays of petunias, fuchsias, geraniums, cyclamen or heather and trailing ivys according to the season.

Prices

London is a capital city and its hotels are therefore more expensive than those in the country. The average price of a hotel in this book is approximately £60 for a double room with private bathroom. Rates are normally inclusive of breakfast and Value Added Tax (VAT) but there are a few exceptions, so you should always ask when making your reservation.

Many visitors coming to London will be seeking that little bit of extra comfort and luxury, or they may be celebrating a special occasion, so we have also included some really exquisite hotels whose rooms could rival those of a far more expensive establishment: such hotels charge in the region of £70-£90 per night for a double room.

Other visitors may require more modestly priced accommodation; we have, therefore, included many hotels where a double room, without private bathroom, is available for £40 or less.

Choosing an Area

One of the first things to decide is where, in this vast city, you wish to stay. We have therefore included a brief 'pen portrait' of the different areas to help readers decide which one most suits their particular needs and priorities.

It has often been said that London is a collection of villages, and this was, indeed, the way the city came into being. This also accounts for its diversity of character and architectural styles.

Because, understandably, many visitors wish to be centrally located, especially if their visit is a short one, we have included the maximum number of hotels in the centre. However, an underground journey of twenty minutes or so can be well worthwhile if it leads to a place of charm and character where the air is sweeter, the restaurants better as well as cheaper and the local pubs are real 'locals' and not simply tourist haunts. We have therefore included hotels in a number of the more attractive outer areas and also in the neighbourhood of Gatwick airport.

Reservations and Special Requirements

If at all possible, make your reservation in advance. You will normally be asked for your credit card number or a deposit to cover the first night's accommodation. Many hotels now accept confirmation by Fax. It is important to confirm prices when booking, ask if breakfast and VAT are included and give as much notice as possible if you have to cancel or change your reservation.

If you have any special requirements, eg ground floor room, baby's cot etc, always mention this when making your booking. Also, if it is at a weekend it is worth enquiring if any special rates are available.

At the back of this book you will find sections for people with disabilities, for establishments where children are made especially welcome and for hotels with easy car-parking.

Complaints

We very much hope you will be happy with the hotel you choose from this guide. However, should you have any cause for complaint, or suggestions for improvement, please do not hesitate to pass them on to the owner or manager, who will usually be only too keen to put things right.

If you have a serious complaint which cannot be settled on the spot, you should contact the London Tourist Board (tel: 071 730 3450) and also write to us. We will follow up all such complaints, but we regret that we cannot act as intermediaries on your behalf, nor can we or the publishers accept responsibility for any of the services or accommodation described. All the establishments are recommended in good faith, but they can change hands or staff and other problems can arise which result in a deterioration of standards. In such cases neither the authors nor the publishers can be held responsible.

Invitation to Readers

We are always keen to hear visitors comments on the establishments in this guide. We also welcome reports on any good places which may have escaped our attention.

Transport in London

Hotels in the Central London section are all within a ten minute walk of the nearest tube station. Those in the

Outer London or Airports sections are often very near a tube station. If this is not the case access will be by bus or British Rail. As detailed travel instructions are included with all entries, you should have no difficulty finding the accommodation of your choice.

The 'Tube', as the underground is known, and buses run from approximately 5.45am to 12 midnight Monday to Saturday and 7.45am to 11pm on Sundays. Note that buses and tubes become very crowded during the rush hours — 7.30-9.30am and 4.30-6.30pm Mondays to Fridays. Avoid travelling at those times if you can, for your own comfort.

Airbuses run from Heathrow Airport to central London every twenty minutes, from approximately 6.30am to 9.30pm daily.

Daily passes or travelcards for the buses, tubes and trains are available. These are valid after 9.30am weekdays and all day at week-ends, at a cost of approximately £3 to cover all services in the central area (Zone 1).

If you are staying in London for four or more days you should purchase a weekly pass or travelcard. These work on a basis of zones and cost about £11 for the centre zone, for example. You can find out about these from any tube or British Rail station or telephone London Regional Transport on 071 222 1234.

Cars

For those coming to London by car we strongly advise finding a hotel with parking (see Parking, page 155-6) then using public transport to get around. To drive or park in central London (except on Sundays) can be quite a nightmare for a resident, let alone a visitor.

INNER LONDON

Bayswater

Bayswater lies north of Kensington Gardens, the more 'manicured' section of Hyde Park west of the Long Water. In the south-west corner of these 275 acres of parkland is situated Kensington Palace, known to many of the royal family who have their London home here as 'KP' (some state rooms and the Court-Dress Collection are open to the public). Here also is the Round Pond where in times gone by nannies used to wheel their charges. These days one is more likely to see local people walking their dogs, or young footballers practising their game, while at weekends model boat enthusiasts take over.

Facing the gardens are some of London's most attractive large hotels, notably White's and the Park Court. Beside them runs Bayswater's most charming street: St Petersburgh Place, its name reflecting the former Russian influence in this part of London, although the three places of worship that remain are Anglican, Greek Orthodox and Jewish.

A few years ago Bayswater's once famous department store, Whiteley's, re-opened its doors to the public after many years of neglect. Beautifully renovated and now housing a large cinema complex and numerous shops, restaurants and cafés, it has once again become the focal point of the area.

However Bayswater, like so many in London, is an area of contrasts: Queensway, which bisects it, is very cosmopolitan and somewhat scruffy as are many of the surrounding streets and squares. This is one of the very few areas of London which has 24-hour opening shops as well as numerous teashops and restaurants of all kinds lining its main thoroughfares. The latter tend to be more in the 'cheap and cheerful' than the gourmet category although there are some good Greek ones and lovers of Indian food say Westbourne Grove has the best selection in London.

On Sundays it makes a pleasant diversion to take a stroll along the Bayswater Road where artists and craftsmen display the works they have for sale on the railings of the park, while a Thursday morning visit to the weekly antiques auction at Phillips in Salem Road is a must for the collector.

Transport is excellent: lots of buses and underground stations at Bayswater (Circle and District lines) and Queensway (Central line).

Places to Visit

Kensington Gardens
Kensington Palace
London Toy and Model
 Museum

Portobello Road Market
Queensway Ice Rink
Serpentine Gallery

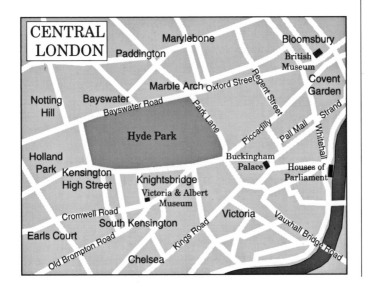

Garden Court

£5 voucher scheme

30 Kensington Garden Square
London W2 4BG
Tel 071 727 8304/071 229 2553
Fax 071 727 2749

Price Band	££
Credit Cards	Access/Visa
Bathrooms	Mainly private
Television	Lounge and in rooms
Breakfast	English style
Telephone	In rooms
Parking	Metered in square

Situated in a leafy Victorian square the Garden Court, one of London's longest established small hotels, has, for many years, represented excellent value in a conveniently central area. A fine building, with interesting architectural detail, its shining white façade and the recent addition of lovely flower boxes in the double porch make it stand out from its neighbours — most of which, by comparison, look in urgent need of a facelift!

All bedrooms have now been pleasingly refurbished with mahogany fitted furniture and bedcovers and carpets that tone with the Wedgewood pattern wallpapers. They have tea and coffee makers and recently installed telephones and hairdryers. Rooms on the top floors are especially imaginative and, for the energetic, well worth the extra climb. Further improvements have been made to the breakfast room and lounge, which doubles as a bar, and is a cosy place to sit and discuss the day's sightseeing with other guests or the friendly owners and staff.

How to get there
Underground to Bayswater, turn left, and take the second left (Porchester Gardens) which leads into Kensington Garden Square.

Byron Hotel

36-38 Queensborough Terrace
London W2 3SH
Tel 071 243 0987
Fax 071 792 1957
Telex 263431 BYRON G

£5 voucher scheme

Price Band	££££
Credit Cards	All major credit cards
Bathrooms	Private
Television	In rooms
Breakfast	Continental and English
Telephone	In rooms
Parking	Difficult

The Byron Hotel is one of the best examples we have ever seen of an imaginative Victorian house conversion. The major part of the ceiling over the reception area has artfully been lowered to provide an extremely elegant non-smoking dining room above.

A wooden buffet surmounted by mirrors runs the length of one wall — guests help themselves to a Continental breakfast. There is waitress service for those who prefer English breakfast. Modern stained glass windows and flower boxes link the dining room with the reception below. There is very attractive rattan furniture.

The lounge and bedrooms are equally delightful — each is different. Great attention has been paid to detail — there is even a rim of gold around the door handles.

At the back of the house is an indoor patio tiled in white and green with large wicker-work chairs, pot plants and arched windows overlooking the garden.

Facilities include individually controlled air-conditioning and heating, a lift, trouser presses, hairdryers and tea and coffee makers. Very highly recommended.

How to get there

Underground to Queensway. Walk along Bayswater Road towards Marble Arch (the park will be on your right) to Queensborough Terrace. The hotel is 300yd on the right.

Kensington Garden Hotel

Kensington Garden Square, London W2 4BH
Tel 071 221 7790 Fax 071 792 8612

Price Band	££-£££
Credit Cards	All
Bathrooms	Private (see below)
Television	In rooms
Breakfast	Buffet
Telephone	In rooms
Parking	Metered in square

What a gem: total refurbishment has created the perfect small hotel which, while retaining the original features of the building, is the essence of warmth and comfort.

The lounge/reception, which is entered on the left of the front door is more like a sitting room in a home than a hotel, with its fireplace filled with dried flowers, chintzy sofas and armchairs that tone.

The fourteen roooms are furnished and decorated in inpeccable taste have hospitality trays, mini-bars and hairdryers. Double rooms have bath tubs as well as showers and are fully tiled in warm peach; all have fluffy towels and complimentary toiletries. Space prohibits three of the single rooms having their own toilet (all have excellent showers), but there are plenty on the landing.

Prices are very reasonable, especially in the off-peak season, considering its convenient location, charm and comfort. Highly recommended.

How to get there

Underground to Bayswater, turn left and take the second left, Porchester Gardens, straight to the hotel.

Bloomsbury

The British Museum stands in the heart of Bloomsbury and epitomises the area as a whole: solidity and respectability are its hallmarks. Consisting largely of elegant, leafy squares and parks surrounded by fine Georgian houses, it is also the home of the University of London and a number of internationally renowned hospitals. Between about 1907 and 1930 it was the base of the Bloomsbury Group — a gathering of prominent philosophers, artists and writers who met here in the houses of Vanessa Bell and Virginia Woolf to discuss aesthetic and philosophical questions in a spirit of agnosticism. Its members also included the novelist E. M. Forster and the biographer Lytton Strachey among many others.

For visitors seeking accommodation in Bloomsbury, the best street to try is Cartwright Gardens. Just 5 minutes' walk from the hustle and bustle of Euston and Kings Cross Stations, this is a quiet crescent of eighteenth-century houses overlooking private gardens, the tennis courts of which are available for use by all guests. Two other very elegant streets of hotels are Montague Street and Bedford Place, both running south from Russell Square. Visitors on a tight budget might like to try the hotels on Gower Street which tend to be more simply furnished. Note that Gower Street is a main thoroughfare, so light sleepers should request a room at the back.

Bloomsbury is within walking distance of West End theatres and the shops of Oxford and Regent Streets. There are plenty of restaurants on Southampton Row, but the more adventurous may like to stroll into Soho where they will find all the best that London has to offer in fine food of all nationalities to suit all pockets.

Transport is exceptionally good in this part of town. As well as Kings Cross and Euston Stations to the north, there is Holborn to the south and Russell Square to the east. Russell Square is particularly convenient for visitors arriving on the Piccadilly Line from Heathrow Airport. The Heathrow Airbus also stops at Russell Square.

Bloomsbury is deservedly one of the most popular centres of visitor accommodation in London.

Places to visit

British Museum

Covent Garden Market

Dicken's House

London Transport Museum

National Gallery

Photographer's Gallery

Pollock's Toy Museum

Soane Museum

Arran House Hotel   £5 voucher scheme

77-79 Gower Street

London WC1E 6HJ

Tel 071 636 2186

071 637 1140

Fax 071 436 5328

Price Band	£-££
Credit Cards	Access/Eurocard/Mastercard/Visa
Bathrooms	Private and shared
Television	In rooms and in lounge
Breakfast	English
Telephone	Public and in rooms
Parking	See below

Over the last few years the Arran House has risen to become one of the best small hotels in Gower Street. The bedrooms have been attractively decorated — they include a particularly pretty cottage-style single room on the top floor and spacious and sunny family rooms overlooking the garden. They all have tea and coffee-making facilities and those on the front have double glazing.

The dining room is most unusual, being decorated with examples of the weaponry of ancient warfare — swords, knives, helmets etc and there is even part of a suit of armour which serves as a lamp-shade!

The staircases have been enlivened with a series of

old playbills and several delightful posters advertising the Green Line coach services of yesteryear. Vases of fresh flowers picked from the hotel's own garden are to be found throughout the house. The garden, with its pink and cream rambling roses and colourful bedding plants is open for guest's use and barbecues are held there in the summer season — it really is an oasis in the heart of the city.

The Arran House is a very welcoming hotel and to make guests feel as much at home as possible the new young managers have provided a microwave oven, a fridge and a coin-operated washing machine and drier for guest's use. Daily newspapers are available at breakfast time. The hotel even has a limited number of parking spaces. These must be reserved in advance and a small charge is payable.

We expect The Arran House to go from strength. Very strongly recommended.

How to get there
Underground to Goodge Street. Cross over Tottenham Court Road and walk along Chenies Street. Turn left into Gower Street and The Arran House is on the left.

Crescent Hotel   £5 voucher scheme

49-50 Cartwright Gardens
London
WC1H 9EL
Tel 071 387 1515
Fax 071 383 2054

Price Band	££
Credit Cards	Access/Eurocard/Mastercard/Visa
Bathrooms	Private and shared
Television	In rooms
Breakfast	English
Telephone	Public
Parking	Difficult

Standing in an elegant eighteenth-century terrace overlooking a park, the Crescent is a peaceful, attractively decorated family-run hotel. The traditional-style lounge with its solid black fireplace and Regency mirror contrast pleasantly with the marbled peach wallpaper on the staircases and the pale pinks and greens of the bedrooms.

Most of the bedrooms have been completely refurbished over the last few years and many of the bathrooms are brand new. Everything literally sparkles and on my visit the mere fragrance of the lillies in the entrance hall would have enticed me to stay were I a tourist!

The breakfast is above average and includes prunes, grapefruit, etc, as well as everything normally expected.

This hotel is of particular interest to tennis players, since the management can arrange access to the courts in the private gardens opposite the hotel and also provides racquets for guests' use. The Crescent is run with professionalism and flair. Highly recommended.

How to get there
Underground to Russell Square (this is ideal for Heathrow Airport). Cross over the road and walk to the end of Marchmont Street. You will see Cartwright Gardens and the Crescent on the left, past the traffic lights.

Haddon Hall Hotel   £5 voucher scheme
39-40 Bedford Place
Russell Square
London WC1B 5JT
Tel 071 636 0026/2474 Fax 071 323 1662

Price Band	££
Credit Cards	See below
Bathrooms	Private and shared
Television	In lounge
Breakfast	English
Telephone	Public
Parking	Difficult

Visitors are attracted to the Haddon Hall by its flower boxes brimming, on my visit, with pink pelargoniums and deep blue trailing lobelia. Run by a Spanish lady, it has an unusually spacious ground-floor lounge and a Spanish-style breakfast room with basketwork chairs and starched white tablecloths. Autumn colours predominate in the bedrooms, there is a drinks vending machine in the hall and the location is ideal for Oxford Street and Theatreland.

Please note that although the hotel accepts all major credit cards, guests presenting discount vouchers are requested to pay by cash. Also note that vouchers are only redeemable on bookings of two nights or more.

How to get there
Underground to Russell Square (ideal for Heathrow Airport). Turn left out of the station, left past the Russell Hotel, right alongside the park and left into Bedford Place. The Haddon Hall is towards the end on the right.

Harlingford Hotel £5 voucher scheme
61-63 Cartwright Gardens
London WC1H 9EL
Tel 071 387 1551
Fax 071 387 4616

Price Band	££
Credit Cards	Access and Visa
Bathrooms	Private
Television	In rooms and lounge
Breakfast	English
Telephone	In rooms
Parking	Difficult

The Harlingford is an excellent, long established family-run hotel. Part of an elegant nineteenth-century terrace king a park, it has gone from strength to strength. itional bathrooms have been installed and new nd pink flowered curtains and matching bedcovers ppeared in the bedrooms. The lounge and dining room have been re-carpeted and hung with beautiful deep pink and blue curtains, complete with swags and tails. On a cold winter's day, the imitation coal fire makes the elegantly furnished lounge a really cosy room in which to relax after a day's sight-seeing.

The bedrooms on the front of the house have good views over the trees and park and there are plenty of shops and restaurants within two minutes' walk.

The atmosphere is friendly and relaxed; the owners enjoy their work and have no difficulty in combining a lot of hard work with a lot of fun. Strongly recommended.

How to get there
Underground to Russell Square (ideal for Heathrow Airport). Cross over the road and walk to the end of Marchmont Street. You will see Cartwright Gardens and the Harlingford on the left, just past the traffic lights.

Hotel Cavendish   £5 voucher scheme

75 Gower Street
London WC1E 6HJ
Tel 071 636 9079

Price Band	£
Credit Cards	None
Bathrooms	Shared
Television	In lounge
Breakfast	English
Telephone	Public
Parking	Difficult

The Hotel Cavendish has been run by Mrs Phillips and her family for almost 40 years now and is the sort of place to which guests return time and again. Everything about the hotel has an air of calm and permanence about it — the dressing tables with their pretty lace cloths, the ornate marble fireplaces and the original built-in dresser which runs the length of one dining room wall. I even saw a most unusual single room which has a series of beautiful stained glass windows and which also looks out onto the leafy back garden.

The dining room is particularly spacious with plenty of colour — pretty yellow tablecloths with matching brown Welsh tapestry mats, lots of pot plants and a display of poppy-design plates.

Prices are amongst the most reasonable in London and currently (1994) stand at £25 for a single and £35 or less for a double room. Good value for money in a central location.

How to get there
Underground to Goodge Street. Cross over Tottenham Court Road and walk along Chenies Street. Turn left into Gower Street and the Cavendish is on the left.

Jesmond Hotel   £5 voucher scheme
63 Gower Street
London WC1E 6HJ
Tel 071 636 3199

Price Band	£
Credit Cards	Access/Eurocard/Mastercard/Visa
Bathrooms	Shared
Television	In lounge
Breakfast	English
Telephone	Public
Parking	Difficult

The Jesmond has more the feeling of a house than many of London's smaller hotels. The dining room, with its cabinet full of books, its colourful Portmeirion pottery and its prints of old London is a welcoming place to start day and the managers obviously enjoy lingering over nversation with their guests. As in most of the Gower Street hotels there is a huge lounge in which to relax after a day's sight-seeing.

The bedrooms are spotlessly clean and comfortable, if simple, with tea and coffee making facilities. Rooms on the back are especially favoured since they overlook the garden.

There are several large rooms, making it particularly suitable for families. The location is good, just two minutes' walk from the British Museum, and prices are among the lowest in London: approx £20 for a single room and £30 for a double.

How to get there
Underground to Goodge Street. Cross over Tottenham Court Road and walk along Chenies Street. Turn left into Gower Street and the Jesmond is on the left.

Jenkins Hotel   £5 voucher scheme

45 Cartwright Gardens
London WC1H 9EH
Tel 071 387 2067
Fax 071 383 3139

Price Band	££
Credit Cards	Access and Visa
Bathrooms	Private and shared
Television	In rooms
Breakfast	English
Telephone	In rooms
Parking	Difficult

The Jenkins is definitely one of the best hotels in Cartwright Gardens. In fact it is so comfortable and welcoming that it is more like a home than a formal hotel. For example, the large country-style kitchen with its scrubbed wooden table, ironing board propped up against the wall and television muttering away quietly to itself, serves as the reception office.

Next door to the kitchen is a pretty little dining room with white lace tablecloths on a background of blue, matching frilled curtains and vases of red carnations dotted here and there.

All the bedrooms are equipped with fridges and tea and coffee making facilities and some have antique gilt mirrors, ornate tiled fireplaces and attractive floral curtains. The hotel overlooks a little park whose tennis courts are open for the use of guests (rackets and balls are available on loan).

Prices are very reasonable, so it is very popular and reservations should be made well in advance.

How to get there
Underground to Euston or Russell Square.
From Euston — turn left into the main Euston Road and take the third street on the right. This is Mabledon Place which leads directly into Cartwright Gardens.
From Russell Square — cross the road into Marchmont Street and a short walk will bring you to Cartwright Gardens on the left, just past the traffic lights.

Mabledon Court Hotel

£5 voucher scheme

10-11 Mabledon Place
London WC1H 9BA
Tel 071 388 3866
Fax 071 387 5686

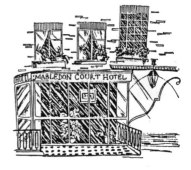

Price Band	££
Credit Cards	Access/Visa
Bathrooms	Private
Television	In rooms
Breakfast	English
Telephone	In rooms
Parking	Difficult

Run with great enthusiasm by the son of Mr and Mrs Davies of the Harlingford Hotel, the Mabledon Court is a modern-style hotel which opened just five years ago. Unlike many of London's small hotels, it has a lift. The bedrooms are equipped with hairdryers and tea and coffee making facilities and other little luxuries, such as complimentary shampoo are to be found in the bathrooms. Decor in the bedrooms and bathrooms is in beige and the latter are tiled throughout. Please note that there are no bathtubs — showers only.

Downstairs there is a cosy lounge with comfy sofas and copies of *The Tatler*. Beside the lounge is a modern dining room with eye-catching limed oak chairs and vases of flowers dotted here and there.

A medium-priced hotel with a warm welcome and every comfort. Strongly recommended.

How to get there

Underground to Euston. Turn left into the main Euston Road and 2 minutes' walk will bring you to Mabledon Place on the right. The Mabledon Court is on the right.

Mentone Hotel

54-55 Cartwright Gardens
London WC1H 9EL
Tel 071 387 3927   Fax 071 388 4671

Price Band	££
Credit Cards	Access, Eurocard, Mastercard, Visa
Bathrooms	Private and shared
Television	In rooms
Breakfast	English
Telephone	Public
Parking	Ask at reception

The proprietor of the Mentone, Mrs Tyner, is a keen gardener and throughout the summer season the hotel looks particularly welcoming with its glorious hanging baskets and its flower boxes brimming with colour.

The Mentone is very much a family-run hotel and it has seen many improvements over the last year or so, including the addition of several well-designed and attractively tiled bathrooms. (Please note that the single rooms do not have private facilities). A number of the bedrooms have been redecorated and tea and coffee making facilities are now available in all rooms.

The hotel is recommended to guests seeking a very quiet room in a central location. Rooms at the front have pleasant views over the little park and tennis courts. Lastly, the prices on a double room at the Mentone are a couple of pounds lower than those of its neighbours and bookings of two or more nights are preferred.

How to get there
Underground to Russell Square. (This is especially convenient if you are coming from Heathrow Airport on the Piccadilly Line.) On leaving the station, cross Bernard Street and walk along Marchmont Street. At the end of Marchmont Street is Cartwright Gardens and the Mentone on the left.

Morgan Hotel

24 Bloomsbury Street
London WC1B 3QJ
Tel 071 636 3735

Price Band	££
Credit Cards	None
Bathrooms	Private
Television	In rooms
Breakfast	English
Telephone	Public/rooms
Parking	Difficult

£5 voucher scheme

The standards of the Morgan Hotel are high: flower boxes always look their best and the glass and brass sparkles.

One of the brothers is a talented carpenter and he has designed and built the hotel's *pièce de résistance* — its charming little dining room. This is an oak-panelled room with a pretty display of china, arrangements of dried flowers and two cosy niches at the end. The air-conditioned bedrooms are furnished in maroon and grey and they all have elegant easy chairs. All windows have double-glazing.

The Morgan Hotel also has a recently opened annexe a couple of doors further up the road with somewhat larger luxury suites which may be booked by longer-stay visitors. The rates for these are extremely reasonable.

The Morgan has an excellent location right beside the British Museum. It is very popular, so make reservations well ahead. Bookings of two nights or more are preferred.

How to get there
Underground to Tottenham Court Road. Walk along Great Russell Street past the YWCA and turn left into Bloomsbury Street at the traffic lights. The Morgan Hotel is on the right.

Ridgemount Private Hotel

65 Gower Street
London WC1E 6HJ
Tel 071 636 1141

Price Band	£
Credit Cards	None
Bathrooms	Shared
Television	In lounge
Breakfast	English
Telephone	Public
Parking	Difficult

The Ridgemount is run by a very friendly Welsh couple who make one feel immediately welcome. A couple of years ago they had the fortune to feature on the front page of the *New York Times Travel Supplement*, which is testimony to their high reputation as a reliable budget hotel.

They have recently acquired the hotel next door and many improvements are currently afoot which will extend and improve the facilities even more.

There is a large comfortable lounge in which a tea and coffee machine has recently been installed.

Bedrooms vary in size and decor and include some large rooms on the back of the house. These rooms are ideal for families since children are made especially welcome here.

Prices are very reasonable, making this one of London's most popular hotels for people travelling on limited funds.

How to get there

Underground to Goodge Street. Cross Tottenham Court Road and walk along Chenies Street. Turn left into Gower Street and the Ridgemount is on the left.

Ruskin Hotel

£5 voucher scheme

23-24 Montague Street
London WC1B 5BN
Tel 071 636 7388
Fax 071 323 1662

Price Band	££
Credit Cards	See below
Bathrooms	Private and shared
Television	In lounge
Breakfast	English
Telephone	Public
Parking	Difficult

Run for many years by the same Spanish family, the Ruskin is a popular hotel located right beside the British Museum. Standards of cleanliness are such that one is reminded of the phrase 'one could eat off the floor'!

A vase of flowers stands on each of the dining room tables which, on my visit, were covered in pale peach-coloured tablecloths which contrasted beautifully with a collection of pot plants standing on the window ledge. The feature of the huge, high-ceilinged lounge is its nineteenth-century mural which depicts cattle grazing peacefully on open land which is now Camden Town! Behind the lounge is a cold drinks machine.

The bedrooms have been equipped with tea and coffee making facilities and hairdryers and those on the front have double-glazing. Some of the bathroom floors are tiled in marble, which is most unusual for a hotel in this price range, and, best of all there is a lift.

Although the hotel does accept all major credit cards, guests presenting vouchers are requested to pay by cash (only redeemable on bookings of two nights or more).

How to get there
Underground to Tottenham Court Road. Follow British Museum signs and turn left into Montague Street. The Ruskin is on the right.

Thanet Hotel

8 Bedford Place
Russell Square
London WC1B 5JA
Tel 071 636 2869/071 580 3377
Fax 071 323 6676

Price Band	££
Credit Cards	Access/ Mastercard/ Visa
Bathrooms	Mostly private
Television	In rooms
Breakfast	English
Telephone	In rooms
Parking	Difficult

Glorious flower boxes draw one like a magnet to the Thanet: a riot of colour against deep blue windows and doors, all sparkling in the warm sunshine. Inside everything is just as fresh, with expensive wallpapers and shining paintwork. The dining room has a pretty maroon and cream carpet, matching tablecloths and a compact breakfast bar at the rear. The varied breakfasts includes peaches, muesli and the special 'Thanet Mixed Grill'.

The bedrooms are bright and the decor is mainly in pastel shades with colourful borders and friezes. As in so many of these Bloomsbury houses, some beautiful tiled fireplaces and antique mirrors are to be found in the bedrooms, all of which have tea/coffee makers and radios.

Expect a warm welcome in this excellent budget hotel just two minutes' walk from the British Museum.

How to get there

Underground to Russell Square (ideal for Heathrow Airport). Turn left out of the station, left past the Russell Hotel, right alongside the park and left into Bedford Place. You will see the Thanet a little way down on the left. (Five minutes' walk).

Chelsea

Originally one of London's riverside villages, Chelsea was for many years famous as an artists' colony, our equivalent of the Paris Left Bank. Sadly, high rents and rates have now forced all but the most successful to seek cheaper romantically situated accommodation and the area has become colonised by the affluent from the world of fashion, show-biz and pop music.

Synonymous with Chelsea is the very long Kings Road, lined with boutiques and restaurants of every description, runing the entire length of the area and a mecca for the young and trendy. One of Chelsea's loveliest streets is Cheyne Walk with some fine examples of Georgian architecture and magical views of the Thames, especially at night-time. Here a handful of artists still live in their colourful houseboats.

Chelsea's most beautiful building is the Royal Hospital, designed by Sir Christopher Wren, and now home to the Chelsea Pensioners, the old soldiers who are a familiar sight in their be-medalled tunics. In late May that feast of colour, scent and achievement — The Chelsea Flower Show — is held in the grounds.

Sloane Square and the area immediately surrounding it is different from the rest of Chelsea, both in its architecture with stately tree-lined streets of tall red-brick houses, and its inhabitants — the 'Sloanes' — highborn, elegant and often very rich. The square itself is a charming mixture of the two cultures with its flower stall and seats under shady plane trees. The Royal Court Theatre shows mainly *avant-garde* plays. Restaurants abound in Kings Road and its environs and range from the supremely elegant to the cheap and cheerful.

Transport
Underground Sloane Square (Circle and District lines) and plenty of buses to all parts of London.

Places to Visit

Carlyle's House
Chelsea Physic Garden
  (summer)

National Army Museum
Royal Hospital

Annandale House

£5 voucher scheme

39 Sloane Gardens
London SW1W 8EB
Tel 071 730 6291

Price Band	£££
Credit Cards	Access/Visa
Bathrooms	Private (except two rooms)
Television	In rooms
Breakfast	Buffet
Telephone	In rooms
Parking	Difficult

Ideally situated, just two minutes' walk from bustling Sloane Square, Annandale House stands in a quiet road of elegant houses fronted by tall plane trees.

Solid and spacious, the furnishings have an old fashioned charm and the atmosphere is one of genuine friendliness. Bedrooms, really large by London standards, contain tea/coffee makers and hairdryers. Breakfasts are very much a feature — different every day of the week — eggs cooked in various ways, Welsh rarebit, kippers and, on Sundays, a special treat, a breakfast tray delivered to your door! Kosher and vegetarian diets are willingly catered for — no bacon or sausages are served.

Annandale House has a loyal clientele of both tourists and business people, so bookings should be made well in advance to avoid disappointment.

How to get there
Underground to Sloane Square, turn left, and Annandale is just two minutes' walk down Sloane Gardens, on the left-hand side.

Covent Garden

Covent Garden, in the heart of London, is one of the city's most fascinating and colourful areas. It was London's principal wholesale market for fruit, vegetables and flowers. After the market was re-housed across the river on a more suitable site, the huge market area (the Piazza) with its nineteenth-century cast iron structure was re-vamped and re-furbished. Now numerous specialist shops, plus a delightful range of open-air stalls, both here and in the surrounding streets, sell arts, crafts, hand-made clothes and jewellery. On Sundays there is a general market and on Mondays it is antiques.

Covent Garden, home of the Royal Opera House and some of the world's most famous theatres, including the Drury Lane, is an area in which to stop, browse, and relax; the latter made easy by the bewildering array of pubs, wine bars, coffee shops and restaurants of every price range and nationality, which spill their tables onto the pavements with enticing colourful displays and delicious smells. Many of London's top restaurants are here but most offer a fixed, and very reasonably, priced 'pre-theatre' dinner, enabling visitors to enjoy gourmet food at an affordable price before the evening rush begins.

Needless to say transportation is superb in Covent Garden; as well as the tube station of the same name (Piccadilly Line) those of Piccadilly Circus and Leicester Square are within a stone's throw, and numerous bus services take visitors to all parts of London.

Places to Visit

Bank of England Museum
British Museum
Guinness World of Records
London Silver Vaults
London Transport Museum
National Gallery

National Portrait Gallery
Museum of the Moving
  Image
Old Bailey
St James's Park
Sir John Soane's House

The Fielding Hotel

£5 voucher scheme

Broad Court
Bow Street
London WC2B 5QZ
Tel 071 836 8305
Fax 071 497 0064

Price Band	££-£££
Credit Cards	All
Bathrooms	Private
Television	In Rooms
Breakfast	Continental (extra charge)
Telephon	In rooms
Parking	Difficult

An attractive eighteenth-century building, with diamond-paned windows and flower filled window boxes, The Fielding stands in a small paved walkway, lit by gas lamps. Push open the door into the cosy little reception, which doubles as a bar. The friendly manager will reserve theatre or opera seats or book sightseeing tours and makes all guests feel cosseted. Unsurprisingly, people return here again and again, as much for this special atmosphere as the unique location, within sight and sound of the Royal Opera House and a minutes' walk of the attractions of Covent Garden. Bedrooms, some in the form of suites with writing desks and armchairs, have theatrical prints adorning the walls and are full of old-world charm. Bathrooms are modern and shining.

The Fielding is understandably popular with many guests booking ahead from one visit to the next, so advance reservations are strongly advised.

How to get there
Underground to Covent Garden. Turn left into Long Acre then right. Bow Street is the third turning right and Broad Court first left.

Earls Court

Earls Court is a cosmopolitan area on the west side of the city especially favoured by Australians. Close to the South Kensington Museums, it is famous for its two vast exhibition centres: Earls Court and Olympia, which play host to numerous world-famous events throughout the year, including Crufts Dog Show, The Ideal Home Exhibition and The Royal Tournament. It is a mixture of noisy streets (Earls Court Road, Warwick Road) and quiet, leafy squares (Nevern Square, Earls Court Square, Courtfield Gardens). There are numerous cheap restaurants offering dishes of equally numerous nationalities.

Generally speaking, the accommodation to be found in Earls Court is of the budget variety and much of it caters specifically for young people and students. Thus we have had to be quite rigorous in our selections for this area and have included only a small number of hotels here.

Places to visit
Brompton Cemetery
Commonwealth Institute
Geological Museum
Natural History Museum
Science Museum
Victoria and Albert Museum

Amsterdam Hotel

£5 voucher scheme

7 Trebovir Road
London SW5 9LS
Tel 071 370 2814/5084
Fax 071 244 7608

Price Band	££
Credit Cards	All
Bathrooms	Private
Television	In rooms
Breakfast	Continental
Telephone	In rooms
Parking	Difficult

The Amsterdam is a well situated and delightful small hotel for discerning visitors. The proprietor is lucky to have a manager whose hobby is needlework and examples of here taste and talent are to be seen all over the hotel.

Bedrooms are welcoming and comfortable, all with tea/coffe-making facilities, hairdriers, soft lighting and pleasing decor. Polular with both parents and youngsters is the family suite on two levels, separated by a little staircase. The *piece de resistance* is the breakfast room: scalloped pink tablecloths and cushions tone with beautiful silk curtains, entirely covering the big bay window with frills and ruffles — yet another example of the manager's expertise.

Secretarial services for business visitors and a lift are added attractions.

How to get there

Underground to Earls Court. Take the Earls Court Road exit and turn left out of the station. Trebovir Road is the first left and the Amsterdam is on the right.

Henley House Hotel

£5 voucher scheme

30 Barkston Gardens
Earls Court
London SW5 0EN
Tel 071 370 4111/ 4112
Fax 071 370 0026

Price Band	££-£££
Credit Cards	All major credit cards
Bathrooms	Private
Television	In rooms
Breakfast	Continental
Telephone	In rooms
Parking	Difficult

Henley House is situated in one of the most pleasant streets in Earls Court, overlooking a shady garden square. The hotel has been completely refurbished over the last year or so, so that visitors passing over its marble steps now enter a beautifully decorated reception area which, with its elegant sofas and expensive curtains, has brought a touch of luxury to this nonetheless very reasonably priced hotel.

The dining room is very pretty too: pink table-cloths, terracotta vases full of dried flowers and ears of corn, silk plants and a tiled fireplace. In the bedrooms, care has been taken to match the attractive blue and pink bedcovers with the friezes on the walls and everything looks fresh, bright and new. Complimentary tea and coffee are available to guests on arrival and tea and coffee making facilities are also provided in all the bedrooms as are hair dryers.

Strongly recommended.

How to get there

Underground to Earls Court. Take the Earls Court exit, cross over and turn right. Barkston Gardens is the first turning on the left and the Henley House is on the left.

London Tourist Hotel

£5 voucher scheme

15 Penywern Road
London SW5 9TT
Tel 071 370 4356
Fax 071 370 7923

Price Band	££
Credit Cards	All
Bathrooms	Private
Television	In rooms
Breakfast	Continental
Telephone	In rooms
Parking	Difficult

Totally refurbished during 1993 the London Tourist Hotel is a great asset to Earls Court. Over the front door is a smart blue and gold canopy and decor everywhere is pleasing and of a high quality.

Especially attractive is the first-floor lounge, built in conservatory style, overlooking private gardens; cane furniture with brilliant cushions and huge potted palms almost touching the ceiling give a delightful summery feel even on a winter's day. There is complimentary tea and coffee and plenty of magazines to read.

Bedrooms are comfortable and well-fitted and bathrooms are fully tiled and sparkling.

In spite of its name this is an especially suitable hotel for business visitors, having a fully equipped room with fax, telex, photocopying and secretarial services as well as a small conference suite. There is also a brand new, highly efficient lift.

How to get there
Underground to Earls Court. Taking the Earls Court Road exit, turn right and the second right is Penywern Road. The hotel is about halfway down on the left.

Nevern Hotel   £5 voucher scheme
31 Nevern Place
London SW5 9NP
Tel 071 370 4827   Fax 071 370 1541

Price Band	£
Credit Cards	Access, Amex, Visa
Bathrooms	Private and shared
Television	In rooms
Breakfast	Continental (English optional extra)
Telephone	In rooms
Parking	Difficult

In the Earls Court area, the Nevern is our recommenda-
tion for people travelling on a tight budget. It is a family
run hotel which stands on a quiet street, just one minute's
walk from the underground station. It is the sort of place
in which guests can always be assured of a warm welcome
— the receptionists have been there for as long as I can
remember, which is always a good sign.

Most of the bedrooms have been redecorated recently
— pink and blue bedcovers against a pale blue and white
wallpaper — and many private and shared bathrooms
have been installed. There is a large, freshly painted
lounge on the ground floor and a little pine-panelled
dining room in the basement. A value-for-money hotel.

How to get there
Underground to Earls Court. Turn left out of the Earls
Court Road exit and a minute's walk will bring you to
Nevern Place on the left. The Nevern Hotel is on the left.

Rushmore Hotel   £5 voucher scheme
11 Trebovir Road
London SW5 9LS
Tel 071 370 6505/3839
Fax 071 370 0274
Telex 297761 Ref 1933

Price Band	££
Credit Cards	All major credit cards
Bathrooms	Private
Television	In rooms, including satellite
Breakfast	Buffet
Telephone	In rooms
Parking	Ask at reception (approx £5 per day)

A highly talented artist has painted all sorts of exotic *trompe l'oeil* scenes on the walls — a ruined Greek temple here, an English country garden there — and has designed each room individually, making an important feature out of the original shutters (some are even painted in black with gold tracery) and adding a wonderful range of colourful curtains, blinds and pelmets.

Each bedroom has a name and corresponding theme. For example, the Ocean Room is a blue room with a liner cruising across one of its walls and an awning suspended from its ceiling, while the Indonesian Room is furnished with exquisite curved rattan chairs, an oriental lampstand and antique desk.

Futon sofa beds are being used to accommodate extra guests — a very sensible idea. All the bedrooms have hairdryers and tea and coffee making facilities.

The dining room and reception are just as beautiful as the bedrooms. The dining room resembles a summer patio and the reception is all fresh flowers, pale yellow wooden panelling and more *trompe l'oeil* paintings.

The addition of a conservatory for breakfast and small functions, and a guests' lounge are added attractions at this constantly improving small hotel.

Prices are competitive — other London hotels in this class normally charge at least £10 per night more. Highly recommended.

How to get there
Underground to Earls Court. Take the Earls Court Road exit and turn left out of the station. Trebovir Road is the first left and the Rushmore is on the right.

Holland Park and Notting Hill

Though one of London's smaller parks Holland Park is still a pleasant place for a stroll especially when the sun is shining and one can appreciate the beautiful plumage of the peacocks that live here. Also open-air plays and concerts are sometimes held here in summer, as well as events for children during school holidays.

Linking it to Notting Hill is Holland Park Avenue, a broad thoroughfare lined with London Plane trees; behind stand some good examples of Georgian architecture.

Notting Hill is a pleasantly cosmopolitan area, some useful shops lining its main road and just a short walk from the famous and colourful Portobello Road Market, best on Saturdays, when hundreds of stalls and little shops vie with each other to offer every kind of 'antique'. While many of these may be no more than a few years old, bargains are certainly to be found and even the non-expert can pick up an interesting oddment which makes an appealing souvenir. Just south of Notting Hill lies Hillgate Village, a pretty area of tiny, though very expensive, town houses, each painted in a different bright colour, and beyond, as the road drops south towards Kensington (Notting Hill is literally on a hill) are some of London's finest residential streets of large and immaculate houses, many of which are now embassies.

Eating places abound; you could try a different cuisine every night without once stepping on a bus or tube.

Transport, also, is excellent with two underground stations: Notting Hill (Central, Circle and District lines) and Holland Park (Central line).

Places to Visit
Holland Park
Kensington Palace
Leighton House
Portobello Road Market

The Holland Park Hotel

6 Ladbroke Terrace
London W11 3PG
Tel 071 792 0216/071 727 5815
Fax 071 727 8166

Price Band	££-£££
Credit Cards	All
Bathrooms	Mainly private
TV	In rooms
Breakfast	Buffet
Telephone	In rooms
Parking	Difficult

Situated in a tranquil tree-lined street, although just moments from the main road, shops and restaurants, this is a small hotel of immense charm and character. The building is a mixture of old and modern, but the two blend perfectly and little stairways and corners highlighted by strategically placed pieces of antique furniture, add to its interest.

The twenty-three bedrooms have been individually designed, each making clever use of colour and space and all boasting excellent beds — some antique mahogany, some brass — tea/coffee making facilities and nice bathrooms complete with fluffy towels and toiletries.

Perhaps, however, the outstanding feature of the Holland Park Hotel is the beautiful drawing room, where antiques and oil paintings and huge windows overlooking a well-tended garden make one imagine oneself to be staying in a country manor.

This hotel, already one of London's top ten, is sure, in the years ahead, to become even lovelier.

How to get there

Underground to Notting Hill. Take the exit to the north side, turn left and after the row of shops Ladbroke Terrace is the first on the right.

Kensington High Street

Kensington High Street and the surrounding areas offer everything the visitor to London could possibly want. While the High Street itself is lined with an enormous variety of shops from department stores to suppliers of artists materials, the side streets are almost exclusively residential. There are charming and peaceful squares within a stone's throw of the bustling shopping area, at their best in springtime when the heavy clusters of flowers, both pink and white, on the ornamental cherry trees turn it into a veritable wonderland.

To the north of the High Street are two streets of note: Kensington Church Street and Kensington Palace Gardens. The former is famed for its antique shops for the serious collector, not the bargain hunter as prices are high. The latter is nicknamed 'Millionaires Row' with some of London's largest and most exclusive residences, many now occupied by embassies. Immediately to the east lies Kensington Palace (the London home of several members of the royal family) and Kensington Gardens remembered fondly by many as the place where spruce, uniformed nannies would walk their young charges, pausing for a gossip on one of the park benches while the offspring of the rich and famous fed the ducks on the round pond.

Transport is very good, as it is on both District and Circle lines and there are many bus routes.

For restaurants stroll northwards to Notting Hill.

Places to Visit
Commonwealth Institute
Holland Park
Kensington Gardens
Kensington Palace
Leighton House
Victorian Institute

Abbey House

11 Vicarage Gate
London W8 4AG
Tel 071 727 2594

Price Band	££
Credit Cards	None
Bathrooms	Shared
Television	In Rooms
Breakfast	English Style
Telephone	Public
Parking	Difficult

Abbey House stands in an immaculate, peaceful, leafy square just moments from historic Kensington Church Street. Built about 1860 for a wealthy Victorian family, it typifies the 'upstairs, downstairs' houses mentioned in the introduction. A bishop and a member of Parliament are past residents and many original features are retained, notably the fine porch flanked by marble columns and the hallway with its ornate ceiling and marble terrazzo floor from where an elegant wrought-iron staircase leads to a lovely first landing with mullioned windows, masses of plants and an antique chair.

Bedrooms are spacious and freshly decorated. Though simple they have washbasins and excellent orthopaedic mattresses on all beds. Outstanding housekeeping, the friendly professionalism of the owners and the superb location add up to a stay that is extremely good value. Thus it is often hard to get a room here; guests are advised to book well ahead to avoid disappointment.

How to get there
Underground to High Street Kensington. Turn right out of the station and cross the busy High Street. Turn left at St Mary Abbotts Church and walk up Church Street. After two or three minutes' walking the road forks — keep right and Vicarage Gate is the second on the right.

Amber Hotel

exham Gardens
London W8 6JN
Tel 071 373 8666
Fax 071 835 1194

Price Band	£-££££
Credit Cards	All
Bathrooms	Private
Television	In Rooms
Breakfast	Buffet
Telephones	In Rooms
Parking	Difficult

What a delight to find a brand new hotel in London! Three former town houses have been transformed into a most charming and comfortable small hotel, which opened its doors for the first time in July 1992.

One is immediately impressed by the primrose yellow exterior and smart front door leading into an attractive reception area with light woodwork and fresh pastel decor. From here a little staircase takes you to the bar where meals can also be taken and champagne is served to visitors on arrival. This is a nice touch and typical of Dutch hospitality as it is owned by a Dutch company, a fact also reflected in the hearty breakfast of fruits, cheeses and cold meats served in the breakfast lounge.

The airy, well-appointed bedrooms all have hairdryers and are reached by an efficient lift. Those at the back are especially nice, facing the garden where functions are held in summer.

The Amber Hotel is highly recommended; the manager and his staff are friendly and helpful and a bonus for the business traveller is a computer and Fax.

How to get there

Underground to Earls Court. Take the exit to Earls Court Road, turn left and after crossing Cromwell Road Lexham Gardens is first right. The Amber Hotel is on your right.

Aston Court Hotel

25-27 Matheson Road
Kensington Olympia
London W14 8SN
Tel 071 602 9954
Fax 071 371 1338
Telex 919208 ASTON G

Price Band	£££
Credit Cards	All major credit cards
Bathrooms	Private
Television	In rooms and lounge. Satellite TV at no extra charge
Breakfast	English
Telephone	In rooms
Parking	Pay and display

The Aston Court is a very comfortable hotel which opened only four years ago. The beautiful reception lounge, the bar and the dining room have been carefully designed to put one immediately in a relaxed frame of mind. Pale peach festoon curtains, elegant sofas and sparkling mirrors form their main feature.

Spacious pink and grey staircases and bedrooms painted in lemon with green friezes are equally soothing. The bedrooms are equipped with irons, hairdryers, tea and coffee making facilities and a mini-bar. The bathrooms are tiled in marble. There is a lift and laundry, and fax services are available.

As the Aston Court is a corner house all the rooms are sunny and bright; also it stands on a very quiet side street.

How to get there

Underground to West Kensington. Turn right out of the station, cross the busy Cromwell Road and walk up North End Road. Turn right at Barclays Bank and walk more or less straight on past a few shops for about 300yd. The Aston Court is on the corner on the left.

Avonmore Hotel

£5 voucher scheme

66 Avonmore Road
London W14 8RS
Tel 071 603 4296/3121
Fax 071 603 4035

Price Band	££-£££
Credit Cards	All
Bathrooms	Private and shared
Television	In rooms
Breakfast	English
Telephone	In rooms
Parking	Pay and display

Under the same ownership for many years and a former winner of the best private hotel in London organised by the AA, the Avonmore is a place guests return to again and again.

Unusually one enters the hotel through a downstairs door, and into a pleasant room where breakfast is served and a cosy well-stocked bar fills one wall.

Bedrooms are spacious and have tea-making facilities and small fridges; those without en-suite facilities share with just one other room. Restful decor is complemented by colour-matched cushions strewn on the beds and soft lighting from wall lights and plenty of lamps.

Bathrooms are large and worthy of a much larger hotel and offer face cloths along with plenty of fluffy towels.

The Avonmore is very convenient for Earls Court and Olympia exhibition centres, while standing in a quiet and peaceful location.

How to get there
Underground to West Kensington, turn right, cross the busy West Cromwell Road, walk along Matheson Road which takes you into Avonmore Road.

Centaur Hotel

21 Avonmore Road
London W14 8RP
Tel 071 602 3857/071 603 5973

Price Band	££
Credit Cards	None
Bathrooms	Ensuite bathrooms or showers
Television	In rooms
Breakfast	English
Telephone	In rooms
Parking	Unrestricted on street

The Centaur, a 2-Crown hotel, is situated close to Olympia, just off the western end of Kensington High Street. It is a small, friendly hotel with a cosy dining room where tea, coffee and sandwiches are available all day.

Over the last two years, nearly the whole house has been re-decorated and I particularly liked the off-white and pale peach wallpaper which has been used in some of the bedrooms. Bedrooms have clock-radios; ironing facilities are available on request.

The Centaur caters for tourists and business people alike (half of its guests are people visiting exhibitions) and is recommended for lone travellers. Children are made especially welcome. Although only a few minutes walk from Olympia it is in a very quiet location.

How to get there

Underground to Olympia or BR to Kensington Olympia — stations are combined. Turn left out of the station and walk beside the Exhibition Centre. Cross the main road and Avonmore Road is opposite. Note: this station closes at 9pm after which use West Kensington. Turn right, crossing West Cromwell Road, and you will see Matheson Road. Walk along here to the end and left into Avonmore Road. Walk on down and around the corner and the Centaur is on the left. (Approx 5 minutes' walk).

Russell Court Hotel

£5 voucher scheme

9 Russell Road
Kensington Olympia
London W14 8JA
Tel 071 603 1222
Fax 071 371 2286

Price Band	£££
Credit Cards	All major credit cards
Bathrooms	Private
Television	In rooms and lounge. Satellite TV at no extra charge.
Breakfast	Continental (English extra)
Telephone	In rooms
Parking	Andy's Car Park opposite (see below)

Overlooking the Olympia Exhibition Halls, yet standing on a quiet street, the Russell Court is a brand new hotel in a very practical location. Catering almost exclusively for business people, it provides maximum comfort and an enormous number of services and facilities. These include a lift, car parking (approx £5 per day), fax, laundry service and room service (sandwiches, pizzas etc). The bedrooms are equipped with hairdryers, trouser presses, irons and ironing boards, tea and coffee making facilities and a mini-bar.

There is a lovely through room on the ground floor with reception at one end, breakfast room at the other and bar in the middle. Colours throughout are in muted pinks and purples, eg in the festoon curtains in the restaurant and in the bedcovers upstairs, and much of the furniture consists of reproduction period pieces.

How to get there

Underground to Olympia. Turn left out of the station and, keeping the exhibition hall on your right, walk up to the main road. Turn left over the railway and left again into Russell Road. The Russell Court is on the right.

Note that Olympia Station closes around 8.30pm on

weekdays and has variable opening hours on Sundays. In that case, take the Underground to High Street Kensington and take a bus.

Vicarage Private Hotel   £5 voucher scheme
10 Vicarage Gate
London W8 4AG
Tel 071 229 4030

Price Band	££ (singles are only £28)
Credit Cards	None
Bathrooms	Shared
Television	In lounge
Breakfast	English
Telephone	Public
Parking	Difficult

The Vicarage is the ideal bed-and-breakfast hotel and fits its name perfectly, standing as it does on a tranquil, tree-lined side street. An elegant curving staircase with wrought iron banisters leads from the pleasant hallway past a wide, sunny, windowsill full of plants to the bedrooms, which have even more the feel of a country vicarage. They are unusually spacious with solid, old-fashioned furniture and flower-sprigged wallpaper.

Since the friendly managers make guests feel really welcome, and since this little hotel charges no more than many with half its charm and character, it is very popular. Reservations should be made well in advance.

How to get there
Underground to High Street Kensington. Turn right out of the station and left at St Mary Abbotts Church. Walk up Church Street, keeping to the right when the road forks. Vicarage Gate is the second street on the right.

Knightsbridge and South Kensington

Knightsbridge and South Kensington, linked by the broad thoroughfare Brompton Road are, after Mayfair, London's smartest areas. Still mainly residential, in spite of enormously high rates, every scrap of space is used to best advantage. The buildings, whether they be homes or offices, tall and palatial or tiny mews cottages, are uniformly well-kept which, combined with an almost total lack of litter in the streets, makes strolling around a great pleasure.

The name of Knightsbridge is synonymous with Harrods, one of the world's largest and most famous department stores. In this vast terracotta building it is said one can buy just about anything on earth; it is certainly possible to spend an entire day here without seeing it all and to get lost many times! Also vast is the complex of museums further along Brompton Road in South Kensington: the Victoria and Albert (Museum of the Living Arts), Natural History, Geological and Science museums are all here, each meriting many hours of the visitor's time. To avoid mental indigestion you may prefer to limit yourself to the one or two which interest you most. A short walk from the museums brings you to the Royal Albert Hall, a huge amphitheatre, built in the nineteenth century, where all manner of public gatherings and concerts are held. The best known are the Promenade Concerts which take place annually from mid-July to-mid September and are so called because of the 'promenaders' — mainly young people who, for a fraction of the price of an ordinary concert ticket can stand and listen to their favourite classical music.

Many architectural styles are represented in this part of London from the Victorian ostentation of the museums and the pure beauty of Brompton Oratory to the charm of the white stucco houses that surround the squares of South Kensington, and the tiny flower-decked mews cottages (formerly stables) behind them. Incidentally the building unanimously voted London's ugliest is also here: Knightsbridge Barracks which was erected in 1970, a low spot in our architectural heritage, and definitely to be hurried past as quickly as possible. Restaurants abound in this area, although prices do tend to be on the high side and visitors may prefer to venture slightly west towards Gloucester Road or Earls Court in search of affordable meals.

One small luxury, however, can be indulged here for there are no two better places to take afternoon tea, that most English of customs, than Harrods and the Hyde Park Hotel. The latter is particularly delightful in summer when the windows of the elegant drawing-room are opened onto Hyde Park.

Transport is exceptionally good; two underground stations; Knightsbridge (Picadilly Line) and South Kensington (District, Circle and Picadilly lines) and numerous buses which serve all parts of the capital.

Places to Visit
Brompton Oratory
Geological Museum
Harrods
Hyde Park
Natural History Museum
Royal Albert Hall
Science Museum
Victoria and Albert Museum

The Claverley Hotel
£5 voucher scheme

13-14 Beaufort Gardens
London SW3 IPS
Tel 071 589 8541
Fax 584 3410

Price Band	££££
Credit Cards	All
Bathrooms	Mainly private
Television	In rooms
Breakfast	English
Telephone	In rooms
Parking	Difficult

Beaufort Gardens, just a stone's throw from Harrods and bustling Knightsbridge, is a quiet cul-de-sac of elegant five storey houses fronted by giant plane trees.

Here is the Claverley Hotel, an oasis of charm and good taste with the atmosphere and style of a country house. The big bay window of the reading room is curtained from floor to ceiling in chintz, walls are wood-panelled and deep leather sofas and armchairs invite one to linger over a cup of tea, coffee or hot chocolate and browse through the stock of books, magazines and daily papers, or write a postcard at the antique writing desk.

The breakfast room is exceptionally attractive: walls softly sponged in yellow ochre are a groundwork for hand-paintings or garlands and fruits recently completed, and the breakfast menu is delicious, including as it does some lesser known, but very English breakfast dishes such as kippers and kedgeree. Each bedroom is different, some have four-poster or canopied beds and all boast antique furniture and plenty of traditional charm.

How to Get There
Underground to Knightsbridge. Take the exit on the south side of the road of the same name, turn left, past Harrods and you will find Beaufort Gardens on your left. The hotel is on the left of the street.

Five Sumner Place Hotel

£5 voucher scheme

5 Sumner Place
London SW7 3EE
Tel 071 584 7586
Fax 071 823 9962

Price Band	£££
Credit Cards	All
Bathrooms	Private
Television	In rooms
Breakfast	Buffet
Telephones	In rooms
Parking	NCP car park 5 minutes' walk

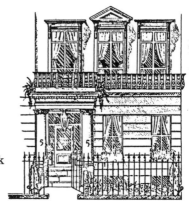

Sumner Place is a joy to walk down at any time of the year; surely one of London's prettiest streets, every house has an immaculate white painted façade and beflowered garden — even in winter when the cyclamen and heathers take over.

A recent (1990) winner of the British Tourist Authority Spencer award for the best bed-and-breakfast hotel in London, No 5 forms part of a lovely terrace, built about 1848, and bears all the hallmarks of that era: a wide porticoed porch and elegant entrance hall, complete with glittering chandelier and huge mirrors.

A lift takes you to the comfortable bedrooms, where warm, soft colour schemes, top-quality curtains and bedcovers and good lighting give a restful effect. Rooms are exceptionally well-equipped with tea/coffe makers, fridges, hair dryers, trouser presses, and even irons and ironing boards.

The high-spot of this hotel is the lovely Victorian conservatory where breakfast is taken. With the sun shining through green plants on to the fresh blue and yellow colour scheme, and plenty of complimentary newspapers and magazines to browse through — what a delightful way to start the day! There are even chairs and tables outside for those who wish to linger a little longer.

How to get there

Take the underground to South Kensington. Turn left at the top of the station steps, cross over at the traffic lights and walk along Old Brompton Road. Sumner Place is the first on the left and you will find the hotel, almost at the end on your right.

The Knightsbridge

£5 voucher scheme

10 Beaufort Gardens
London SW3 1PT
Tel 071 589 9271
Fax 071 823 9692

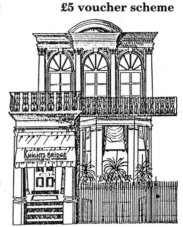

Price Band	££££
Credit Cards	All
Bathrooms	Private
Television	In rooms, including satellite
Breakfast	English style
Telephone	In rooms
Parking	Difficult

Standing in a leafy, traffic-free roads in the fashionable area from which it takes its name, the Knightsbridge is a useful addition to this guide for visitors seeking supreme comfort in a wonderful location.

The reception area is panelled in limed oak, apricot silk draped curtains are matched when possible by flowers of the same colour, and a small fireplace adds charm.

By the time the lift has whisked you to your room the TV set is already welcoming you in your own language! This facility can also be used to book theatre tickets, etc; a most exciting innovation.

Bedrooms are very well appointed; hairdryer, trouser press, mini-bar and hospitality tray are standard, while the most luxurious rooms feature jacuzzis in the fully tiled bathrooms.

Decor is similar throughout with pastel colour schemes and light wood furniture.

Service is quiet and discreet, while additional facilities include secretarial services for business guests and a small health club equpped with exercise machines and a most inviting spa bath.

How to get there
Underground to Knightsbridge, taking the exit on the south side of Knightsbridge Road. Turning left past Harrods, Beaufort Gardens is on the left. The hotel is on the left of the gardens.

Knightsbridge Green Hotel
159, Knightsbridge
London SW1X 7PD
Tel 071 584 6274
Fax 071 225 1635

Price Band	££££
Credit Cards	All
Bathrooms	Private
Television	In rooms
Breakfast	English or Continental (extra charge)
Telephone	In rooms
Parking	Difficult

The Knightsbridge Green Hotel in many ways resembles the kind of excellent small city-centre hotel one finds in continental cities such as Paris or Rome, having simply its entrance foyer on the ground floor, from where one takes the lift to the upper floors. On the first is the delightful Club Room; quiet (all double-glazing is super efficient here) and full of colour, it contains two comfortable sofas, a table with the latest glossy magazines and quality newspapers, little antique writing desk and, in a corner, an inviting display of fresh coffee and cakes set out for guests to help themselves.

Fourteen of the twenty-six rooms are in the form of

suites, each with a sitting room, as well as comfortable bedroom and luxurious bathroom. Note that the latter have tubs and hand showers, not American type showers. A wide choice of breakfast dishes, all served in the rooms up to 10am, adds to the feeling of luxury, as does the ice-machine. The Knightsbridge Green is run with the friendly professionalism that is the hallmark of a good hotel and is superbly located, overlooking Hyde Park and just moments from Harrods and Knightsbridge station, so perfect for Heathrow Airport and theatreland.

How to get there
Underground to Knightsbridge, take the crossing in front of you to the Scotch shop, turn left and you will see the canopy of the hotel in front of you.

Hotel 167

£5 voucher scheme

167 Old Brompton Road
London SW5 0AN
Tel 071 373 0672/3221
Fax 071 373 3360

Price Band	££-£££
Credit Cards	Access, Visa
Bathrooms	Private
Television	In Rooms
Breakfast	Continental
Telephones	In rooms
Parking	Difficult

A distinctive grey-green corner building, just entering the Hotel 167 one immediately notices that this is a hotel with style. The breakfast room/reception is furnished with marble tables, wrought-iron chairs and huge modern paintings, while the hall and stairways, in shades of grey form a perfect introduction to the bedrooms which are full of colour and light. Venetian blinds let in the sun's rays while retaining privacy and efficient double-glazing ensures tranquility on this busy road.

Eclectisism really works here; attractive pieces of antique furniture blend perfectly with modern colour schemes, while king-size beds and dimmer light switches add to the romantic atmosphere and tea/coffee making facilities and mini-fridges increase the feeling of comfort and cosseting so important to tourists and business people alike. The owner and staff of the 167 are friendly yet professional and the location excellent; highly recommended.

How to get there
Underground to Gloucester Road. Turn right, walk down the road of the same name until you reach Old Brompton Road. Right again and you will see the 167 in a corner position on the opposite side.

Swiss House Hotel
171 Old Brompton Road
London SW5 0AN
Tel 071 373 2769/ 9383
Fax 071 373 4983

Price Band	££
Credit Cards	Access/Visa
Bathrooms	Private and Shared
Television	In rooms, also satellite
Breakfast	Buffet
Telephone	In rooms
Parking	Difficult

£5 voucher scheme

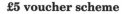

Ivy trailing over white balconies and pretty flower boxes welcome guests to the charming Swiss House. Inside the impression of a country hotel continues: hallways are ρeted in soft russet and apricot walls form a backdrop masses of dried flowers, while plenty of mirrors give a ₂eling of space.

Bedrooms are decorated in restful colours, mainly pinks and greys, many with canopied beds and all with quality bedcovers, attractive furnishings and double-glazed windows ensuring a good nights sleep on this busy road. Everywhere the charming small touches bear witness to the good taste of the owners.

The breakfast room, recently redecorated in fresh blue and white with matching china and, again, dried flowers, contains a fine Welsh dresser where the buffet breakfast of fruit, cheeses, croissants, etc is displayed. Room service snacks, ranging from sandwiches to lasagne are available from noon till 9pm. Swiss House is a delightful small hotel where guests are really made to feel 'at home' so it is naturally very popular; advance reservation are, therefore, strongly advised. Very highly recommended

How to get there
Underground to Gloucester Road. Turn right down the road of the same name till you reach Old Brompton Road. Right again and you will see the Swiss House on the opposite side of the road.

Uptown Reservations
50 Christchurch Street
Chelsea
London SW3 4AR
Tel 071 351 3445
Fax 071 351 9383

Price Band	££-£££
Credit Cards	Eurocard/ Mastercard/ Visa
Bathrooms	Private, but not always attached to bedrooms
Television	Request on booking if required
Breakfast	Continental
Telephone	By arrange- ment with host
Parking	Difficult

As its name suggests, Uptown Reservations is actually a booking agency rather than an individual hotel. It is a new company which has brought together some fifty beautiful private homes, offering bed and breakfast in London's most exclusive areas. Because the accommodation offered is of a very high standard, while the prices are very modest (particularly for a single room), it has been decided to include this agency in this guide.

A typical Uptown property is in Knightsbridge, Chelsea or South Kensington. It will have just one or two guests' rooms, may be furnished with exquisite antiques and might be owned by an interior designer or an art dealer. There may be a pretty patio brimming over with flowers, a conservatory, or even a roof garden. You would stay in surroundings more usually associated with London's grandest hotels at a fraction of the cost.

If you make reservations note that you will be staying in someone's home and there will be certain differences to a hotel. Non-smoking accommodation is available and there is a small supplement for booking only one night.

Very highly recommended, especially for those travelling alone.

Marylebone and Marble Arch

Marylebone, the area lying due north of Oxford Street is an extremely convenient location for both the business and holiday traveller. Theatreland is but a stone's throw away while for those planning a shopping spree the elegant small shops of Bond Street and South Molton Street are within easy walking distance. These are infinitely preferable, in our opinion, than the endless and somewhat scruffy Oxford Street, formerly London's premier shopping street, which, though now pedestrianised has somehow 'gone down' in recent years with the modern preference for boutiques and shopping malls.

It is convenience, rather than any special charm which makes Marylebone such a good choice for the visitor. Vestiges remain of the village it once was — notably Marylebone Lane and the delightful St Christopher's Place, a little walkway of restaurants and boutiques which is at its most magical at Christmas time. Running parallel is James Street, with a string of small restaurants which spill their tables onto the pavement in true continental style, whenever the sun decides to make an appearance!

Marylebone is not, in the main, a residential area. Many of what were once homes are now offices and a large section is devoted to the medical profession — Harley Street being famous the world over for housing the consulting rooms of Britain's most eminent doctors.

Green spaces are somewhat few and far between; sadly Montagu and Manchester Squares, though attractive, are private and, therefore, fenced off from the public. Joggers should fear not, however, as Hyde Park is quite near, just beyond Marble Arch and, to the north of the area, Regents Park is also worth a visit, especially in June and July when Queen Mary's Rose Garden is quite a sight to behold.

An entertaining diversion, on a Sunday, is to visit the

famous Speaker's Corner at Marble Arch where anybody can stand up, usually on an wooden box and say just about whatever they please, provided it is within the law (hopefully!). Depending on world events of the moment these views can be rivetting, amusing, irritating or just plain crazy — but it is definitely not to be missed.

Marylebone has plenty of restaurants, especially in James Street and St Christopher's Place, while for the more adventurous there is the Swedish 'Garbo's' or the Afghan Caravan Serai.

Transport is, of course, outstandingly good with four underground stations and bus services too numerous to mention running to all parts of the capital and beyond.

Places to Visit

Laserium
Madame Tussauds
Planetarium
Regents Park

Regent's Park Open Air
  Theatre (summer only)
Speaker's Corner
Wallace Collection

The Bickenhall Hotel

119 Gloucester Place
London W1H 3PJ
Tel 071 935 3401
Fax 071 224 0614

Price Band	£££ - ££££
Credit Cards	All
Bathrooms	Private
Television	In Rooms
Breakfast	English Style
Telephones	In Rooms
Parking	Difficult

The extensive refurbishment recently carried out on the Bickenhall Hotel has transformed this fine Georgian building into an attractive and comfortable small hotel while losing nothing of its original character.

Even the façade stands out from its neighbours, painted in an unusual, but pleasing, shade of pale grey.

The wide hallway contains a little fireplace and is carpeted in blue with a fleur-de-lys pattern, while the walls beneath the dado are painted to match. This unusual and attractive carpet extends into the spacious lounge where deep sofas beckon and wall lights flatter the fresh turquoise and white of the decor.

A beautiful and ornate staircase, as well as a lift, lead to well-appointed bedrooms, all fitted with tea/coffee making facilities, hair-dryers, trouser-presses and remote control satellite television. Wall lights and fitted mahogany furniture are standard but each floor has a different colour-scheme which adds character.

The Bickenhall Hotel is an excellent choice for the business man or lady as typing and Fax services are available and reception staff are happy to make travel arrangements, theatre and car-hire bookings etc. There is also room or lounge service for drinks and snacks.

How to get there
Underground to Baker Street. Take the exit into Marylebone Road, which you cross by an underpass, then turn right into Baker Street, which you also cross and Bickenhall Street brings you out almost in front of the hotel.

Edward Lear Hotel

30 Seymour Street
London W1H 5WD
Tel 071 402 5401
Fax 071 706 3766

Price Band	£££
Credit Cards	All
Bathrooms	Private and shared
Television	In rooms
Breakfast	English
Telephone	In rooms
Parking	Difficult

The Edward Lear Hotel wins top marks for both charm and location. From the terrazzo-floored little entrance hall there is a choice of two lounges: one is quiet with a writing desk and armchairs, the other, complete with Austrian blinds and matching deep sofas, contains the reception desk, television, and shelves full of books for guests to borrow. The breakfast room, also on the ground floor, is furnished with Windsor chairs and has a polished wood floor for practicality. The main colour is a lovely warm coral and menus on the tables exhort guests to 'Eat, relax and enjoy' — what a pleasant way to start the day!

Stairways, carpeted in russet, lead to comfortable, cosy bedrooms all fitted with tea/coffee makers and clock-radios.

Children are especially welcome at the Edward Lear. There are cots and high-chairs for guests to borrow and many young visitors have contributed to the artists' gallery of drawings on the theme of Edward Lear, the famous writer of nonsense verse, who once lived in this house.

Not surprisingly both this and its sister hotel the Parkwood are extremely popular so reservations should be made well in advance to avoid disappointment.

How to get there
Underground to Marble Arch. Turn right and immediately right again into Great Cumberland Place. Seymour Street is the second cross street and you will see the Edward Lear almost straight in front of you.

Four Seasons Hotel   £5 voucher scheme
173 Gloucester Place
London NW1 6DX
Tel 071 724 3461/071 723 9471
Fax 071 402 5594

Price Band	££
Credit Cards	All
Bathrooms	Private
Television	In Rooms
Breakfast	Buffet style
Telephones	In Rooms
Parking	Difficult

The Four Seasons Hotel is very well located: Madame Tussauds and Regents Park are within a short walk and the famous Lords Cricket Ground and Oxford Street shops just a stones' throw away. Cricket enthusiasts will also be interested to walk around the corner into Dorset Square, where the first match was played last century.

Public areas and bedrooms are painted in light colours and the fresh feeling is enhanced by plenty of green plants dotted around. In the style of many of these townhouse hotels breakfast is taken in a pretty conservatory which also has a little lounge, furnished with white painted cane furniture upholstered in pinks and greens.

How to get there
Underground to Baker Street. Take the side exit into Baker Street, which you cross, walk along Melcombe Street into Gloucester Place where, after turning right, you will see the hotel on the opposite side of the road.

Hadleigh Hotel

£5 voucher scheme

24 Upper Berkeley Street
London W1H 7PF
Tel 071 262 4084
Fax 071 723 8469

Prices	££
Credit Cards	All
Bathrooms	Private
Television	In rooms
Breakfast	Continental (extra charge)
Telephone	In rooms
Parking	Difficult

Very well located, just moments from Marble Arch, the Hadleigh really stands out from its somewhat shabby neighbours, with its smart exterior enlivened by window boxes. The interior comes as even more of a pleasant surprise; the hall and stairways are decorated in cool blues and greys with spotlights picking out strategically placed photos of stage and movie stars.

Bedrooms, spacious and comfortable with uncluttered decor, have mini-bars, tea/coffee making facilities and large glass-topped tables for the breakfast which is delivered to your room.

The manager, who sits at a little reception on the first floor, is most friendly and helpful and room rates are excellent value for such a central location.

How to get there
Underground to Marble Arch. Turn right, then first right into Great Cumberland Place. The third crossroads is Upper Berkeley Street and you will see the Hadleigh on the opposite side of the road.

Hallam Hotel

£5 voucher scheme

12 Hallam Street
London W1N 5LJ
Tel 071 580 1166
Fax 071 323 4527

Price Band	£££-££££
Credit Cards	All
Bathrooms	Private
Television	In Rooms
Breakfast	English
Telephones	In Rooms
Parking	Difficult

The Hallam Hotel is superbly situated in a quiet street, just moments from Oxford Circus. From the steps one looks through the attractive doorway, flanked by lamps, to the pleasing interior. On the right, as you enter, the lounge/reception is as inviting for the friendly welcome one receives as it is for the lovely deep armchairs, upholstered in blue velvet, and the quality curtains.

Bedrooms have recently been refurbished to a very high standard and no expense has been spared to make them as comfortable as they are charming; colours of peach and turquoise predominate in the wallcoverings, curtains and bedspreads. The feeling of luxury is enhanced by remote-control television, mini-bars, hair-dryers and tea/coffee making facilities — there is also a lift. Especially popular are the three tiny single rooms known as cabins which are very reasonably priced.

The breakfast room has wall-lights and pink table cloths and overlooks a tiny patio with plants — 'a bit of green in the centre of London' as the owner says.

We highly recommend this lovely little hotel to anyone who wants to stay in a central location, yet in a quiet and friendly atmosphere. Like all the best places it fills up very quickly so bookings should be made well in advance.

How to get there
Underground to Oxford Circus. Take the exit to the nor
side of Oxford Street, walk along Upper Regent Stree
bearing left at All Souls Church into Portland Place. A
right-hand turn into New Cavendish Street brings you
into Hallam Street just opposite the hotel.

Hart House   £5 voucher scheme

51 Gloucester Place
London W1H 3PE
Tel 071 935 2288
Fax 071 935 8516

Price Band	££
Credit Cards	Access, Amex, Visa
Bathrooms	Mainly Private
Television	In rooms
Breakfast	English
Telephones	In Rooms
Parking	Difficult

Hart House is typical of the upstairs/downstairs houses
mentioned in the introduction. Ceilings are high with
fine mouldings and both public areas and bedrooms are
spacious. The latter have recently been refurbished and
all contain tea and coffee making facilities and remote-
control televisions. Tranquility is ensured by efficient
double-glazing which is most important as traffic on
Gloucester Place is quite heavy.

The enthusiastic young owner of Hart House, who
has recently taken over from his parents, has made many
improvements, such as the smart striped wallpaper in
the entrance hall and refurbishment of the old world
style breakfast room. The impeccable housekeeping that
is its hallmark has been retained; indeed one is quite
dazzled by the shine on the paintwork and gleam on the
windows.

An excellently located small hotel for those to whom being 'in the centre' is most important. Three underground stations (Marble Arch, Bond Street, and Baker Street) are within a short walk, as are the stops for buses to just about every attraction in London.

How the get there
Underground to Marble Arch. Turn left along Oxford Street and left again into Portman Street which leads into Gloucester Place; Hart House is about five minutes' walk further on the left-hand side.

Hotel Concorde

50 Great Cumberland Place
London W1H 8DD
Tel 071 402 6169
Fax 071 724 1184

Price Band	££££
Credit Cards	All
Bathrooms	Private
Television	In Rooms
Breakfast	Continental (English extra)
Telephone	In rooms
Parking	Difficult

The first thing one notices at the Concorde are the bright blue window blinds and the little trees and carriage lamps that flank the front door.

Public areas are elegant. Delicately striped wallpaper forms a perfect background to Regency tables, one topped by an attractive dried flower arrangement in an antique china teapot. The lounge, where afternoon tea is served, and the small bar are equally lovely; leather armchairs, large table-lamps, attractively-lit paintings and masses of antiques give the feeling of being in a private home. Bedrooms are comfortable but simpler with built-in furniture.

The Concorde is friendly and traditional. Bathrooms have tubs rather than showers and tea is brought to your room instead of making it yourself which is the norm nowadays. The presence of a lift is an added bonus, as is the fact that guests may use the restaurant and larger bar in the sister hotel, the Bryanston Court, next door.

How to get there
Underground to Marble Arch. Turn right and Great Cumberland Place is the first right. You will find the Concorde on your right.

Hotel La Place

£5 voucher scheme

17 Nottingham Place
London W1M 3FB
Tel 071 486 2323
Fax 071 486 4335

Price Band	££££
Credit Cards	All
Bathrooms	Private
Television	In rooms, including satellite
Breakfast	English style
Telephone	In rooms
Parking	Difficult

Hotel La Place has the unique distinction of being the only small London hotel known to us to have recieved a Four Crowns Commended from the English Tourist Board. This is deserved for the guests' comfort and convenience are paramount here and the great range of facilities include a lift, ice machine, restaurant and bar. A piano stands in the corner of the bar, furnished with cane chairs and little twinkling lights set in exotic greenery; obviously a happy meeting place for family, friends and guests alike.

No expence has been spared with the exquisite bed-rooms, which boast orthopaedic mattresses (some king-size), seating areas, mini-bars, hospitality trays, hairdryers and trouser presses. Some rooms are in the form of suites and are an excellent choice for business visitors.

Decor everywhere is pleasing and of a high quality. Antique lace curtains covering the windows make a refreshing change from the ubiquitous nets.

Superbly located and run with friendly professional-ism, it is not surprising that Hotel La Place is so popular; bookings should, therefore, be made well in advance.

How to get there
Underground to Baker Street. Taking the Marylebone Road exit, cross this main road by the underpass and turn left. Nottingham Place is the second street on the right and the hotel is also on the right — a total of five minutes' walk.

Parkwood Hotel   £5 voucher scheme
4 Stanhope Place
London W2 2HB
Tel 071 262 9484
Fax 071 402 1574

Price Band	£££
Credit Cards	Access/Visa
Bathrooms	Mainly private
Television	In rooms
Breakfast	English
Telephone	In rooms
Parking	Difficult

Surely occupying one of the best situations in London, the Parkwood is a gracious small hotel. Though only five minutes' walk from busy, noisy Marble Arch it is a world away in this quiet street which opens onto all the splendour of Hyde Park.

The front door opens into an attractive hallway and thence the charming lounge with its pink sofas, plants and candy striped wallpaper. Many of the bedrooms have recently been re-decorated with pretty papers and prints and all have satellite television, radio-alarms and tea/coffee makers. Some rooms are non-smoking. Bathrooms are nice though a little old-fashioned, having tubs and hand-showers, not power showers.

The Parkwood is under the same ownership as the Edward Lear as one notices by the same coral walls in the breakfast room, the hand-written menus exhorting one to 'Eat, relax and enjoy' and even the artists' gallery of paintings by visiting children. Evening meals are also available here.

Once again a very, and deservedly, popular small hotel, so we urge prospective visitors to book early, if possible.

How to get there
Underground to Marble Arch. Turn right and after crossing the main Edgware Road, Stanhope Place is the first turning right. You will see the Parkwood Hotel on your left.

Regents Park Hotel

156 Gloucester Place
London NW1 6DT
Tel 071 258 1911
Fax 071 258 0288

Price Band	£££
Credit Cards	All
Bathrooms	Private
Television	In rooms
Breakfast	Continental (English or Singapore at extra charge)
Telephone	In rooms
Parking	Difficult

Like its sister hotel the Knightsbridge, Regents Park Hotel is a new and pleasing addition to this guide.

The reception area has been smartly refurbished and a huge mirror over the fireplace reflects glittering chandeliers, soft draped curtains and masses of flowers, real and artificial.

Breakfast is taken in the conservatory where a number of interesting dishes from Singapore could make an exciting change.

Bedrooms all have identical decor; light wood furniture is complemented by pastel colour schemes, tea/coffee makers and well-fitted bathrooms.

Business visitors are well catered for with fax and photocopying facilities, while the cocktail bar and restaurant are open to non-residents; excellent for entertaining friends and business associates.

How to get there

Underground to Baker Street. Take Baker Street exit, cross the road, turning right. Take first left past Melcombe Street and the hotel is on the right.

Paddington

Paddington is the area due north of Hyde Park whose focus is the railway station of the same name. Many improvements are being made in this area and Norfolk Square (on which The Camelot Hotel stands) has been freshly laid out with new railings, paths, shrubs and benches, while ambitious plans are afoot to develop the canal basin to the east of the station.

The Paddington hotels are especially recommended to children and to motorists. To children because of the proximity of Hyde Park and to motorists because Sussex Gardens is the only street of hotels in central London to offer limited car parking on a private slip road.

Hyde Park is a paradise for adults and children alike. The lake in its centre which is known as the Serpentine has boating and swimming in summer; there are open-air cafés, a good play park and an Italian Garden with fountains and plenty of hungry waterfowl. Last, but not least, there is the delightful statue of Peter Pan, immortalising in bronze the boy who never grew up.

Restaurants in the area tend to be of the cheap and cheerful rather than the gourmet variety. If they are not to your taste, take a stroll to the Greek and Indian restaurants in Westbourne Grove or to the continental teashops in Queensway.

There is any number of hotels in Paddington and we have had to make our selection here very carefully. This is because the majority of the establishments in this area are either huge, characterless tourist hotels of uneven quality, or smaller hotels which could only be termed disreputable. However, by consulting *Small Hotels of London*, you will be able to find a choice of both simple budget hotels at around £40 per night and some really beautiful luxury hotels at approx £70 per night for two people.

Paddington is very close to the shops in Oxford Street

and has excellent transport services. From the main line station fast trains run to Bath and Oxford which are good destinations for day trips. There are four underground lines — Metropolitan, Bakerloo, District and Circle — and it is possible to pick up the Central Line at Lancaster Gate and outside the Great Western Hotel on Praed Street. The Airbus A2 from Heathrow also stops at Lancaster Gate. For drivers, Paddington lies immediately off the A40(M) and the A5.

Places to visit
Church Street Market
Hyde Park
Little Venice
London Toy and Model Museum
Queen's Ice Rink
Speaker's Corner

Adare House
153 Sussex Gardens
Hyde Park
London W2 2RY
Tel 071 262 0633

Price Band	£-££
Credit Cards	None
Bathrooms	Private and shared
Television	In rooms and lounge
Breakfast	English
Telephone	Public
Parking	Difficult

Pretty flower boxes, a sparkling blue front door and a freshly painted façade are a good indication that the Adare is one of Paddington's best budget hotels.

The owners, Mr and Mrs O'Neill, work very hard to

keep standards high and over the last year or so have re-carpeted the staircases and a number of the bedrooms. Nearly everywhere has been redecorated — Regency stripe wallpaper in the entrance hall and mainly pastel shades in the rest of the hotel. Six private bathrooms have been added and the bedrooms now have tea and coffee making facilities and hairdryers. The dining room is traditional in style with crisp white tablecloths and green and white crockery.

The Adare is recommended to guests who wish to be assured of clean, comfortable accommodations while travelling on limited funds.

How to get there
Underground to Paddington. On leaving the station, walk along London Street past the Royal Norfolk Hotel. When you reach Sussex Gardens cross over and you will see Adare House behind the trees.

Camelot Hotel

£5 voucher scheme

45-47 Norfolk Square
London W2 1RX
Tel 071 723 9118
/071 262 1980
Fax 071 402 3412

Price Band	££-£££
Credit Cards	Access Visa
Bathrooms	Mainly private, some rooms with shower only
Television	In lounge and rooms
Breakfast	English
Telephone	In rooms
Parking	Difficult

Built in 1850, the Camelot is a beautifully restored town-house hotel of great charm, one of the very best hotels in its category in London. The reception area forms an integral part of the lounge (a feature which one finds only too rarely) so that guests immediately have a sense of belonging. The lounge is furnished with two enormous floppy sofas; there is an attractive Victorian tiled fireplace and an antique gilt mirror at the far end. Facing the guest is a lovely vase of yellow lillies.

The halls and stairways are carpeted throughout in warm russet, pleasantly offsetting the light-coloured walls which are hung with a series of antique and modern prints. There is a lift to all floors and bedrooms are very modern with wooden desks, stylish curtains and tea and coffee making facilities. One room even has a four-poster bed and many have views over the quiet garden square.

However, our favourite room is the breakfast room, with its exposed brick walls, large open fireplace and curious 'wooden pictures'. Difficult to describe in words, these three-dimensional representations include a chicken sitting proudly on her eggs, a golfer in plus fours and a sheaf of corn advertising Walton's Mill. One wall is devoted to the paintings of children who have stayed here over the years. A fun room and a great place to start the day.

A very special hotel with efficient, relaxed management.

How to get there
Underground to Paddington. Make you way to London Street and you will soon see Norfolk Square on the left. The Camelot is at the far end on the right. The Heathrow Airbus stops at nearby Lancaster Gate.

Cecil Court Hotel

16 Sussex Gardens
Marble Arch
London W2 1UL
Tel 071 262 3881

Price Band	£
Credit Cards	None
Bathrooms	Shared
Television	In rooms
Breakfast	English
Telephone	Public
Parking	Limited (see below)

Fresh paint and spotless cleanliness are the hallmarks of this little budget hotel with just thirteen bedrooms. Situated very close to the shops of Oxford Street and Edgware Road, it is a good choice for visitors wishing to save as much money as possible.

The decor is mainly in contrasting greens — a deeper patterned green for the carpets and a pale green with a little border for the curtains. In the dining room a varnished pine ceiling and a large mirror over the chimney breast complement the whites and greens of the carpets and tablemats.

Bathrooms are tiled throughout and are naturally spotless. There are a couple of parking spaces in front of the hotel which are available at no extra charge if reserved in advance.

A reliable budget hotel, especially good for motorists.

How to get there

Underground to Edgware Road. Walking towards Marble Arch, you will soon come to Sussex Gardens. The Cecil Court Hotel is on the right.

Delmere Hotel   £5 voucher scheme

130 Sussex Gardens
Hyde Park
London W2 1UB
Tel 071 706 3344 Fax 071 262 1863

Price Band	££££
Credit Cards	All major credit cards
Bathrooms	Private
Television	In rooms
Breakfast	Continental (English optional extra)
Telephone	In rooms
Parking	NCP Car Park nearby

The Delmere is an elegant town-house hotel standing on a tree-lined avenue close to Hyde Park. Run with great enthusiasm by the owners, it has received a Certificate of Distinction by the British Tourist Authority.

It has a beautiful lounge with deep, comfortable sofas, silk flowers and even a little library. The restaurant, La Perla, is open for breakfast (this includes yogurt, croissants, cheeses etc as well as traditional items) and for dinner Mondays to Saturdays inclusive.

Bedrooms are very comfortable — We particularly liked one on the top floor with its gabled roof, pretty frilled curtains and pink side lamps. There is a cosy bar tucked away at the back of the house and every imaginable facility and service is available. To mention but a few — lift, individual safes, fax, laundry, etc.

On top of all this the Delmere also offers special weekend rates, so enquire when making your reservation.

A professionally run, fun hotel suited to business people and visitors alike.

How to get there
Underground to Paddington. Walk along London Street and left into Sussex Gardens. The hotel is on the left. The Heathrow Airbus stops at Lancaster Gate, 5 minutes' walk away.

Europa House

151 Sussex Gardens
Hyde Park
London W2 2RY
Tel 071 723 7343
Fax 071 224 9331

Price Band	£
Credit Cards	Access, Eurocard, Mastercard, Visa
Bathrooms	Private
Television	In rooms
Breakfast	English
Telephone	Public
Parking	Limited parking (see below)

The Europa House represents exceptionally good value for money for visitors seeking budget accommodation whilst not wishing to forgo the comfort of a private bathroom. Currently (1994) a single room with facilities is only £32, and a double £45 for the same.

The rooms are, as one would expect, fairly simply furnished, but they do have tea and coffee making facilities. Irons and hairdryers may be loaned from reception and car parking is usually available if booked in advance (no charge).

The Europa has been run for many years now by the various branches of a large Spanish family and, like most Spanish people, they pay particular attention to their flower boxes, so the hotel has a welcoming façade.

Good budget accommodation.

How to get there

Underground to Paddington. Walk along London Street past the Royal Norfolk Hotel and turn left into Sussex Gardens. You will see the Europa House on the right behind the trees.

Fairways Hotel

£5 voucher scheme

186 Sussex Gardens
London W2 1TU
Tel/Fax 071 723 4871

Price Band	££
Credit Cards	Access, Mastercard, Visa
Bathrooms	Private and shared
Television	In rooms
Breakfast	English
Telephone	Public
Parking	Limited parking on forecourt

Owned by the same family for over 15 years, the Fairways Hotel bears a very pleasant resemblance to a country hotel. Most of the guests have been coming regularly for years, as witnessed by a string of mementos — origami from Japan, crucifix from Jerusalem, etc — lining the walls. We once called here at the beginning of the festive season and the dining room, decorated with Christmas tree, crackers, poinsettias and even special red and white tablecloths embroidered with holly and Father Christmases looked really beautiful.

The bedrooms are also pretty and include one room in pink with a four-poster bed and another with co-ordinated blue and white wallpaper, bedcover and curtains.

The owners of Fairways obviously put a great deal of hard work into ensuring that both guests and premises receive the care and respect which they deserve. Strongly recommended.

How to get there

Underground to Paddington. Take the Praed Street exit, walk along Spring Street and left into Sussex Gardens. Fairways is immediately around the corner on the left.

Gresham Hotel

116 Sussex Gardens
Hyde Park
London W2 1UA
Tel 071 402 2920
Fax 071 402 3137

Price Band	£££
Credit Cards	All major credit cards
Bathrooms	Private
Television	In rooms. Also satellite TV
Breakfast	Continental (English optional extra)
Telephone	In rooms
Parking	Free if reserved in advance

The Gresham Hotel, named after Sir Thomas Gresham, founder of the Royal Exchange, London's first official stock exchange, is one of the very best hotels in the Paddington area. Opened only recently, every item of furniture, every lamp, every fixture and fitting has been carefully chosen to create a series of beautiful, luxurious rooms.

The elegant reception with its polished granite floor and its antique prints of the original Royal Exchange leads into a cosy little bar (drinks are available 24 hours a day) and this again leads into the guests' lounge furnished a little bit in the style of Louis XV. The dining room has unusual green cane-backed chairs and pretty pink table-cloths — a lovely place to start the day.

The colour schemes in the bedrooms vary from floor to floor — all the windows are exquisitely dressed with designer fabrics and most have swags and tails. Limed oak doors and wardrobes are a feature of the bedrooms which not only have hairdryers and tea and coffee making facilities, but also safes for guests' use.

There is a lift to all floors and the reception is manned 24 hours a day.

This is one of London's best hotels in the £££ category — very, very highly recommended, not only for its decor, but also for its excellent management and friendly, efficient receptionists.

How to get there
Underground to Paddington. Go along London Street and turn left into Sussex Gardens. The Gresham is on the left. The Heathrow Airbus stops at Lancaster Gate, 5 minutes' walk away.

Mitre House Hotel

180 Sussex Gardens
London W2 1TU
Tel 071 723 8040/7778
Fax 071 402 0990

Price Band	£££
Credit Cards	All
Bathrooms	Private
Television	In rooms, including satellite
Breakfast	English
Telephone	In rooms
Parking	Plenty on forecourt

£5 voucher scheme

Although the Mitre House has grown over the years from just one house to quite a large hotel, its justification for inclusion here is that in all other respects it is the perfect 'small' hotel. Owned and run by the same family for more than thirty years, the welcome must be one of the warmest in London, and the two brothers who run it and their delightful hand-picked staff immediately become friends.

The reception, lounge and bar are spacious and relaxing, while tea or coffee are available twenty-four hours a day.

The bedrooms, reached by lift, are comfortable and well decorated, especially popular being the spacious family suites.

This is one of our favourite hotels; friendly, welcoming and constantly improving, it is a particularly good choice for motorists, families or those travelling alone who might feel lost in this big city.

How to get there

Underground to Paddington. Take the exit to Praed Street, turn left, then left again into Spring Street and the hotel will be seen on the left.

Alternatively: underground to Lancaster Gate, turn left into Westbourne Street, then right into Sussex gardens and the hotel is across the road.

Note that Airbus A1 stops at Lancaster Gate.

Queensway Hotel   £5 voucher scheme
147-149 Sussex Gardens
Hyde Park
London W2 2RY
Tel 071 723 7749
Fax 071 262 5707

Price Band	£££
Credit Cards	Access/Amex/Diners/Visa
Bathrooms	Private
Television	In rooms
Breakfast	English
Telephone	In rooms
Parking	Limited parking on private slip road

Run by Mrs Anderson and her family for over 20 years, the Queensway is one of our favourite small hotels. Consistently high standards are maintained, while at the same time lots of laughter is generally to be heard amongst family and staff — a great combination.

Decor in the reception area is in soft pinks and blues. An attractive mirror and wood coffee table reflects the ceiling cornices and other wall mirrors reflect strategically placed plants and huge, glittering table lamps. The dining room is similarly luxurious with pink and white tablecloths, Victorian-style spoonback chairs and lots of modern prints lining the walls.

Bedrooms are very comfortable and are equipped with tea and coffee making facilities, trouser presses and hairdryers. Some of the bathrooms are even more spacious and light than those of a 3-star hotel. Four of these include jacuzzis which add that little extra touch of luxury. There is a lift to all floors. Highly recommended.

How to get there
Underground to Paddington. Walk along London Street past the Royal Norfolk Hotel. Turn left into Sussex Gardens and the Queensway Hotel is on the right behind the trees. The Airbus from Heathrow stops at nearby Lancaster Gate.

Victoria

Victoria seems to have become an area of budget accommodation mainly due to the presence of its enormous station which handles visitors travelling both via Gatwick Airport and via the continental boat-trains. London's main coach station is also located in Victoria.

Most of the so-called 'Victoria' hotels are actually situated either in Pimlico or in Ebury Street which is on the very edge of Belgravia. While Victoria has little to recommend it apart from the neo-Byzantine Westminster Cathedral, squashed between McDonalds and a shop, Pimlico and Belgravia both have very disinct characters.

Pimlico is an area of big, white, terraced houses now converted into flats and hotels. A number of Spanish and Italian families live in the area, evidence of which is to be found in the delicatessens, restaurants, shops and market stalls around Tachbrook Street, Denbigh Street and Warwick Way which form the district's focal point.

Belgravia is one of London's richest residential quarters. Like Pimlico, it also consists of solid white Victorian terraces, though here they are even more imposing. Tucked away behind the terraces lie a series of charming cobbled mews, the balconies of which are brimming over with brightly coloured flowers and trailing plants. Also hidden among the mews houses are some very cosy little pubs including the Grenadier and the Grouse and Claret.

Many countries have their embassies in Belgravia and it is very conveniently located for the fashionable shops of Sloane Street and the Kings Road.

Places to Visit

Buckingham Palace	Royal Mews
Guards' Chapel	St James's Park
Guards' Museum	Tate Gallery
Houses of Parliament	Westminster Abbey
Queen's Gallery	Westminster Cathedral

Cartref House

£5 voucher scheme

129 Ebury Street
London SW1W 9QU
Tel 071 730 6176

Price Band	££
Credit Cards	Mastercard/Visa/Amex
Bathrooms	Mostly private
Television	In rooms
Breakfast	English
Telephone	Public
Parking	Difficult

Cartref House is one of the cosiest, most welcoming little hotels in central London. Great attention is paid to detail and each floor has its own colour scheme. The first floor, for example, is decorated in soft blues and white, with patterned bedcovers complementing blue curtains and blue woodwork. All rooms have tea-makers and a couple of easy chairs.

There is a pretty little dining room furnished with Windsor chairs, chequered tablecloths, ornaments and pictures. A very popular hotel, so book well in advance to avoid disappointment. Note that vouchers are accepted only for stays of more than one night.

How to Get There
Underground or train to Victoria. From the station forecourt turn left into Buckingham Palace Road. Walk along a little and turn right into Eccleston Street and then left into Ebury Street. Cartref House is on the left.

Collin House

104 Ebury Street
London SW1W 9QD
Tel 071 730 8031

Price Band	££
Credit Cards	None
Bathrooms	Mainly private
Television	None
Breakfast	English
Telephone	Public
Parking	Difficult

Collin House is a really good small hotel, just 5 minutes' walk from Victoria Coach and Railway Stations. It is warm, welcoming and spotlessly clean and the Welsh owners always make guests feel 'at home'. Bedrooms are of a good size and prettily furnished — light-coloured walls and attractive duvet covers with traditional patterned carpets.

The modern dining room with its little pine tables and benches is hung with a series of enlarged photographs of the family on holiday in Wales — Tintern Abbey, the children at play, the rugged Welsh coastline, etc.

Prices at The Collin House are very reasonable, particularly on the single rooms with full bathroom, currently running at £34.

How to Get There

Underground or train to Victoria. Turn left out of the station forecourt and walk along Buckingham Palace Road, turning right into Lower Belgrave Street. Turning left into Ebury Street, you will soon come to Collin House on your right.

Ebury House

102 Ebury Street
London SW1 9QD
Tel 071 730 1350/1059

Price Band	££
Credit Cards	Eurocard, Mastercard, Visa
Bathrooms	Shared
Television	In rooms
Breakfast	English
Telephone	Public
Parking	Difficult

Ebury House is one of the best small hotels in Ebury
Street. The owner manager has very high standards and
is constantly redecorating, so that visitors can always be
assured of having a fresh, bright room. One particularly
nice room we saw has soft pink and white wallpaper
combined with deep pink duvets and curtains. A pretty
flowered frieze runs around the ceiling and even the
mirror has a special patterned border.

The pine-panelled walls of the dining room are hung
with all sorts of mementos — Coronation cups, a Welsh
dragon, a copper-relief of the Sydney Opera House, etc.

A cosy little hotel where guests can expect a warm
welcome.

How to Get There

Underground or train to Victoria. From the station forecourt turn left into Buckingham Palace Road and then
right into Lower Belgrave Street. Turn left into Ebury
Street and you will soon see Ebury House on the right.

Elizabeth Hotel

37 Eccleston Square
London SW1V 1PB
Tel 071 828 6812

Price Band	££-£££
Credit Cards	None
Bathrooms	Mainly private
Television	In lounge and in most rooms
Breakfast	English
Telephone	Public
Parking	Meters in front of the hotel

The Elizabeth is one of Victoria's best and most popular hotels, mentioned in countless guidebooks and having won an award from the British Tourist Authority as one of London's best hotels in its class. It certainly stands out from its neighbours with its pretty cream paintwork and its favourable position, facing onto the lovely gardens of Eccleston Square, where guests may relax or play tennis if they wish.

The hotel has recently been enlarged into an adjoining property to provide more rooms and a lift. The public rooms are most pleasing, spacious and furnished in a slightly old-fashioned style, which gives a feeling of permanence.

The Elizabeth has a loyal and devoted clientele, so potential guests should write well in advance to avoid disappointment.

How to get there

From Victoria Station walk past the Grosvenor Hotel and take the second left over Elizabeth Bridge. After a few hundred yards you will see the Elizabeth Hotel on the right.

Hamilton House Hotel   £5 voucher scheme

60 Warwick Way
London SW1W 1SA
Tel 071 821 7113
Fax 071 630 0806

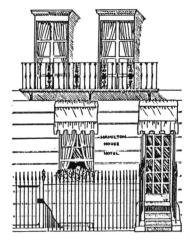

Price Band	££-£££
Credit Cards	Access/Visa
Bathrooms	Mainly private
Television	In rooms
Breakfast	English
Telephone	In rooms
Parking	Difficult

In a convenient location, on the corner of Warwick Way and Belgrave Road, with a solid Victorian façade enlivened by orange window blinds, Hamilton House is the popular choice for may visiting the Victoria area.

The reception is painted in an attractive shade of willow green, echoed in the carpet and complemented by colourful prints on the walls.

Bedrooms have been updated recently to include tea and coffee makers and hairdriers. Rooms at the front have efficient double glazing to ensure a restful night's sleep.

Hamilton House is a well-run, reasonably priced hotel with a long established tradition of service and friendliness.

How to get there

Train or underground to Victoria. From inside the railway station take the escalator to Victoria Place. Walk straight ahead, through the shops, to the exit to Belgrave Road. Turn left and after five minutes' walk Hamilton House will be seen on the corner.

Ivy House

18 Hugh Street
Victoria
London SW1V 1RP
Tel 071 834 9663

Price Band	£
Credit Cards	Amex/Mastercard/Visa
Bathrooms	Shared
Television	Jn rooms
Breakfast	Continental
Telephone	Public
Parking	Difficult, except at weekends

The Ivy House is one of the most modestly priced little hotels in the Victoria area (£30-£35 for a double room, depending on the time of year). It stands in a fairly quiet street of indifferent hotels, and originally took our attention because of its particularly attractive window boxes.

Naturally, at these prices, the bedrooms and bathrooms are very simple. However the hotel has recently been taken over by an enthusiastic young couple who are busy decorating, providing new curtains, bedspreads, etc, and it is expected to go on improving over the next year or two.

Tea and coffee are available on all floors and the continental breakfast is ordered by intercom and brought to your room.

Note that reservations of two nights or more are requested to qualify for the voucher scheme.

A budget hotel with a friendly welcome.

How to Get There

From Victoria Station, walk along the Buckingham Palace Road past the Grosvenor Hotel and turn left over Eccleston Bridge. Hugh Street and Ivy House are on the right.

James House

£5 voucher scheme

108 Ebury Street
Belgravia
London SW1 9QD
Tel 071 730 7338

Price Band	££
Credit Cards	Access/Eurocard/Mastercard/Visa/Amex
Bathrooms	Private and shared
Television	In rooms
Breakfast	English
Telephone	Public
Parking	Difficult

James House is a really cosy family hotel: on my visit children were happily playing with a computer in the pretty little dining room which looks onto a wall covered in colourful hanging baskets and pot plants. Around the dining room are photographs of the children, displays of crystal glasses, fresh lace curtains etc.

The bedrooms are mainly decorated in pink with green vanity units and louvred doors to the wardrobes and showers. Tea and coffee making facilities are provided and hairdryers are available on request. There is a five-bedded room with an attractive (and very solid) bunk bed which would be ideal for families.

Strongly recommended. Note that vouchers are only accepted for stays of two nights or more.

How to Get There
From Victoria Station ask for the Grosvenor Hotel and walk up Lower Belgrave Street which lies opposite it. Turn left into Ebury Street and James House is a few hundred yards down on the right.

The Windermere Hotel

142/144 Warwick Way,
London SW1V 4JE
Tel 071 834 5163/5480
Fax 071 630 8831

Price Band	££-££££
Credit Cards	Access/ Amex/Visa
Bathrooms	Mainly Private
Television	In Rooms
Breakfast	English
Telephone	In Rooms
Parking	Difficult

£5 voucher scheme

The recent enlargement of the Windermere Hotel is of great good fortune to travellers who want to stay near Victoria, as this pleasant hotel really stands out from its neighbours.

Situated on a street once known as the Abbotts Lane because it connected Westminster Abbey with the abbotts residence, the exterior is appealing; lovely lamps flank the front door, green plants fill the window boxes and the railings are even tipped with gold.

Large windows, double-glazed for quietness, allow plenty of light into this corner building and everywhere is fresh and sparkling.

There is a small, relaxing lounge and the attractive dining room, furnished with Windsor chairs, pink table-cloths and pretty rose patterned china adorning the tables, serves very reasonably priced evening meals as well as an excellent breakfast and tea, coffee and snacks at any time.

The price range of the bedrooms is explained by the fact that a few basic rooms remain, while at the top end of the range are the superior rooms which have added extras such as mini-fridges, trouser-presses, hair-dryers, king-size beds in the doubles and bath tubs as well as showers.

The outstanding feature of the Windermere is the friendly professionalism with which it is run and the warm welcome extended to all guests. Not surprising, therefore, that it won an award from the British Tourist Authority in 1991 and is highly acclaimed by the RAC.

How to get there
Underground or train to Victoria, and from the station forecourt turn left into Buckingham Palace Road. Take the first left, Belgrave Road, then the first right, Hugh Street, walk the entire length of this street, turn left at the end and you will see Windermere Hotel on the corner.

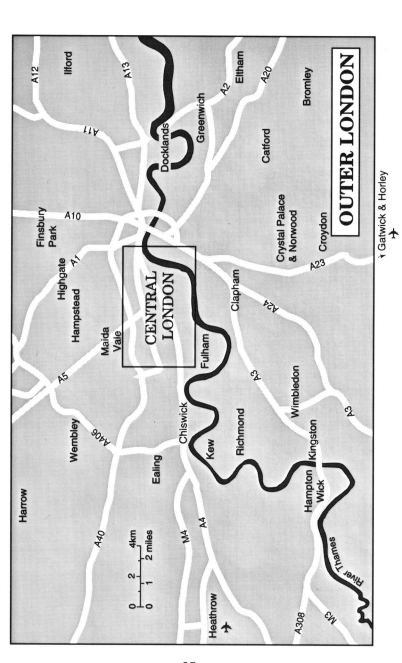

OUTER LONDON

CENTRAL LONDON

↓ Gatwick & Horley

95

OUTER LONDON

Bromley

Bromley is a thriving business and residential centre lying some 8 miles south-east of central London. It is also an important shopping centre with major department stores and a brand new indoor shopping mall.

Much of the town is relatively modern, but there are two buildings of particular historical interest: the seventeenth-century Bromley College or Almshouses which now accommodate retired clergymen and their families and the Bromley Civic Centre which is the former palace of the Bishops of Rochester, dating from the eighteenth century.

On the west side of the town you will find the beautifully landscaped Church House Gardens, the fifteenth-century flintstone tower of the parish church and the modern Churchill Theatre and Library Complex, opened by Prince Charles in 1977.

The best means of transport to Bromley from central London is via British Rail train from Victoria. There is a frequent service and journey time is approximately 20 minutes. For drivers, the A21 passes straight through the town and the Kent countryside and Channel ports are easily accessible.

Places to Visit
Beckenham Place Park
Churchill Theatre
Chislehurst Caves
Elmstead Woods
Sundrige Park

Blyth Hotel

2 Blyth Road
Bromley
Kent BR1 3RX
Tel/Fax 081 464 3785

Price Band	££
Credit Cards	Access/Visa
Bathrooms	Nearly all private
Television	In rooms
Breakfast	English
Telephone	In rooms
Parking	Private car park

A vine carefully trained along their conservatory roof is an indication of the Spanish origins of Mr and Mrs Rodriguez, the owners of the Blyth Hotel. And indeed Mr Rodriguez has a sense of humour, for he has hung a couple of bunches of plastic grapes among the vine leaves to impress guests, lest his own should fail to come to fruition in our greyer climes!

The hotel has eighteen bedrooms, ranging from a pretty pink bedroom in a log cabin at the end of the garden to a large family room with bay window at the front of the house. There is a tea and coffee making machine, ironing facilities, and a bar where drinks are available in the evenings.

The Blyth is very close to Bromley's shops and the town centre is just a five-minute walk.

How to get there
British Rail from Victoria to Bromley South and then a short taxi ride. For drivers, the Blyth Hotel lies immediately off the A21 London Road.

Grianan Hotel

23 Orchard Road
Bromley
Kent BR1 2PR
Tel 081 460 1795

Price Band	£
Credit Cards	None
Bathrooms	Mainly shared (two private)
Television	In rooms and in lounge
Breakfast	English
Telephone	Public
Parking	Private car park

The Grianan, under the management of an enthusiastic young couple, is our selection for budget accommodation in the Bromley area.

The houses in this part of Bromley were built for the very rich some 100 or so years ago, evidence of which is to be seen in the larger than normal entrance hall, bathrooms and kitchen. In fact at one stage the house belonged to a close friend of Sir Frank Whittle, the inventor of the jet engine, and there are several mementos to him in the bar, including a series of photographs of early aeroplanes and some original designs.

Being a detached house, the bedrooms and upper hallways are particularly bright; the dining room overlooks the garden and has a mirror running the length of one wall.

The surrounding streets are very pleasant to stroll along and Sundridge Park lies very close by.

How to get there
Take the British Rail train from Victoria to Bromley South, from where it is only a short taxi ride.

Catford

Catford lies in south-east London, not far from Black-heath and Greenwich. It is a residential and shopping centre, known mainly for its Greyhound Racing Stadium. In terms of entertainment it has both a cinema and a theatre in the form of Lewisham Town Hall which puts on various shows throughout the year. Ladywell Turkish Baths and swimming pool are close by, parking is not a problem and there is a little park very close to our recommended B&B hotel for this area, so it would be a good choice for families.

Although the town itself has little of great historical interest, it is within easy reach of a large number of particularly interesting tourist attractions (see below).

Transport from the centre of London is either from Charing Cross to Catford Bridge station or from Black-friars to Catford station. Journey time in each case is only 15 minutes.

Places to Visit
Beckenham Place Park
Churchill Theatre
Crystal Palace Park
Cutty Sark
Dulwich Park
Dulwich Picture Gallery
Horniman Museum
National Maritime Museum
Nunhead Cemetery
Old Royal Observatory
Ranger's House
Royal Naval College

Mr & Mrs Broughton

31 Ringstead Road
Catford
London SE6 2BU
Tel 081 461 0146

Price Band	£
Credit Cards	None
Bathrooms	Shared
Television	In rooms. Also cable TV (50 channels)
Breakfast	English
Telephone	Public
Parking	Unrestricted on street

Strictly speaking, Mrs Broughton's establishment, standing on a quiet residential street and with just five bedrooms, is more of a B&B than a hotel, but it has been included it for a number of reasons. Firstly, because it is so cheap — £20 for a single and £30 for a double room — and if visitors wished to save money by staying a little outside the centre this would be the ideal place. Secondly, because of its beautiful front and back gardens, brimming over with bright red geraniums, old-fashioned hollyhocks and miniature palm trees — barbecues are held here in the summer. And thirdly, because of the warm welcome guests are certain to receive here.

At such low prices, the bedrooms are naturally quite simple, but they are all very quiet and all have tea and coffee making facilities, although some do not have wash basins. Those overlooking the glorious back garden are especially favoured.

This little B&B is for the hard-nosed bargain hunter!

How to get there
Take the British Rail train from Charing Cross to Catford Bridge (only 15 minutes). Turn left out of the station onto Catford Broadway and then left again at Barclays Bank. Ringstead Road is then the second turning on the right.

Chiswick

Chiswick, situated to the west of London, is barely twenty minutes from the city centre by tube and is a popular residential area for those who, while wishing to live in a conveniently central location, wish also to breathe the clean fresh air one associates with the countryside, for here the town really meets the country and green open spaces abound.

From the busy high road with its usual shops, banks and restaurants run quiet tree-lined streets of Edwardian houses standing in flowery, well-tended gardens. Two areas of note: Bedford Park, a square mile of beautiful detached houses, erected around the turn of the century as a model for all future suburbs and a popular spot for architects and architectural students to visit, and the river frontage at Chiswick Mall and Strand on the Green, two delightful stretches of Georgian houses. The latter has the added benefit of two atmospheric old pubs, one of which is also a restaurant.

Two artists of note have lived in Chiswick: Hogarth, the seventeenth-century satirist, whose house can be visited and Camille Pissaro, the impressionist, who painted some enchanting scenes in the area.

There is a good selection of restaurants and wine bars on the High Road and transport is no problem with two underground stations, Stamford Brook and Turnham Green (District Line) and buses which serve both central London and some beautiful spots to the west such as Kew Gardens and Hampton Court.

Motorists have few parking problems here and Heathrow Airport can be reached in under twenty minutes, either by car or tube.

Places to Visit

Chiswick House	Kew Gardens
Hogarth's House	Kew Bridge Steam Museum

Chiswick Hotel

73 High Road
London W4 2LS
Tel 081 994 1712
Fax 081 742 2585

Price Band	£££ - ££££
Credit Cards	All
Bathrooms	Private
Television	In rooms
Breakfast	Continental. English extra charge
Telephone	In rooms
Parking	On forecourt

Set a little back from Chiswick High Road, behind a line of trees, the freshly painted Chiswick Hotel manages to be both conveniently located and quiet.

The interior, also, has recently been tastefully refurbished, retaining the original Victorian features, such as the mouldings and roses on the high ceilings, and combines them cleverly with up-to-date colour schemes. There is a small bar next to the dining room, where dinner is available from Monday to Thursday.

Well equipped bedrooms have excellent beds, some king-size, and tea/coffee making facilities. Some are on the ground floor, an added bonus for those with heavy luggage or who do not fancy a climb.

Chiswick Hotel also features some attractive apartments, ranging from one to three bedrooms and available on a nightly or weekly basis. These provide a useful alternative for guests who like plenty of space or who like to cater for themselves. Fax, dry cleaning and laundry services are useful extras, especially for business people.

How to get there

Underground to Turnham Green. Turn left along Turnham Green Terrace onto the High Road. Left again and the hotel is about five minutes' walk, on the opposite side. Airbus A2 stops outside.

Clapham

Clapham is an ideal place for visitors to stay when visiting London, especially if they are travelling by car. The South Circular Road (A205) bisects the area and it is only a mile or so from the A23 to Gatwick Airport. There are three underground stations, all on the Northern Line, and Leicester Square is only 15 minutes away.

The centrepiece of Clapham is the Common, which stretches almost a mile from one side to the other and which is at its best on a sunny autumn day. Around Clapham Common Station are clustered some good delicatessens, butchers, gift shops, etc as well as 'Tea Time' — one of London's best known tea shops, and a recently opened cinema showing up-to-the-minute films at half West End prices. There are also plenty of grocers, restaurants, banks, etc on the edges of the Common.

Places to Visit

Battersea Park

Dulwich Picture Gallery

Horniman Museum

Wimbledon Tennis Museum

The Windmill on the Common

Clapham Common South Side
London SW4 9ED
Tel 081 673 4578 Fax 081 675 1486

Price Band	£££-££££
Credit Cards	All major credit cards
Bathrooms	Private
Television	In rooms, also Sky
Breakfast	English
Telephone	In rooms
Parking	Private car park

The Windmill on the Common is our best new entry for 1994/5. It is one of a small number of pubs in London to offer top quality accommodation with all modern conveniences: tea/coffee makers, hairdryers, trouser presses, etc — all in the atmosphere of a country house hotel.

The pub itself is a beautiful mellow yellow-brick eighteenth-century building, decorated summer and winter with glorious flower boxes. It lies on the edge of the Common, so nearly all its bedrooms have wide open views over the ponds, trees and parkland, while the underground station is a mere 5 minutes' walk away.

The pub offers all that one could desire: real coal fires, sophisticated decor, a conservatoty room for families, an aquarium, quality wines by the glass as well as by the bottle, and superb pub grub (average main course £4.50) both at lunch time and in the evenings. On Monday evenings an opera singer provides free entertainment.

The hotel is a new wing to the side of the pub, with its own entrance. Bedrooms are luxurious and there is even a delux 'Canopy Room' with its own mini-bar for those special occasions. Babies' cots are available on request.

The restaurant is a cosy, beautifully decorated, wood-panelled room, open to non-residents as well as guests for breakfast and dinner. Breakfast choices include kippers, yogourt, porridge, black puddings, etc, as well as bacon and eggs. A high chair is available for children.

Prices are lower at weekends than during the week — ask if there are special rates for more than two nights.

A terrific welcome completes the picture — it is the best accommodation for miles around and yet only 20 minutes from the West End.

How to get there

Underground to Clapham Common. Take the exit marked Clapham Common/Clapham High Street. With Lloyds on your left, walk along South Side with the Common on your right. After a few minutes you will see the Windmill on the right.

Croydon

In the midst of recession, Croydon remains a thriving centre of business and commerce, the home of many leading national and international companies. The main shopping streets buzz with life, often made merrier with impromptu entertainment from popular buskers and jazz musicians.

More entertainment is on offer at the Fairfield Halls, a complex which comprises a concert hall, theatre, function room, art gallery, restaurant, etc, and which hosts all sorts of events from plays and craft shows to ballet and wrestling. Around the Fairfield Halls rise tall modern office blocks where the town's wealth lies. By contrast, amid the bustling shops are the Whitgift Almshouses, founded in the sixteenth century and still in use today.

A little to the west of the town centre lies the medieval Croydon Palace, which is now a girls' school; south of the town, in Purley Way, is the Water Palace, one of Europe's largest indoor leisure pools, where the temperature is guaranteed not to drop below 84°F.

East Croydon is the town's main station from which fast and frequent services operate between Central London, Gatwick Airport and the South Coast. For drivers, the borough is bisected by the A23 London/Gatwick Airport/Brighton Road.

Places to Visit
Chartwell
Chessington World of Adventures
Crystal Palace
Hever Castle

Central Hotel
3-5 South Park Hill Road
Croydon
Surrey CR2 7DY
Tel 081 688 5644
Fax 081 760 0861

Price Band	££
Credit Cards	Access/Visa/Amex/Switch
Bathrooms	Private
Television	In lounge and in rooms
Breakfast	English
Telephone	In rooms
Parking	On hotel forecourt

Lying in a quiet residential street, the Central Hotel stands out from neighbouring houses in that it is painted in an unusual burnt sienna and covered with attractively contrasting deep green ivy.

Inside the reception doubles as a bar and both the lounge and dining room overlook a pretty little garden full of shrubs and small trees. The hotel serves a modestly priced evening meal (approx £7) and the menu includes specialities such as venison in red wine and Cajun chicken. It also caters for parties, business meetings and wedding receptions, etc.

The nineteen bedrooms are all individually decorated, including one with a four-poster bed with pretty lace curtains. They all have tea and coffee making facilities, trouser presses and hairdriers.

It is just a 15 minute walk from the hotel to Croydon's main shopping centres and the Fairfield Halls.

How to get there
British Rail from Victoria to East Croydon, then a short taxi ride. For drivers the Central lies just off the A212 Coombe Road.

Kirkdale Hotel

22 St Peter's Road
Croydon, Surrey CR0 1HD
Tel 081 688 5898 Fax 081 680 6001

Price Band	£-££ (reduced weekend rates)
Credit Cards	Access/Visa
Bathrooms	Private
Television	In rooms and lounge
Breakfast	English
Telephone	In rooms
Parking	Private car park

In autumn the immaculate façade of this pretty little hotel is covered in glorious deep red Virginia creeper. Inside there is the cosy lounge a Victorian tiled fireplace, piles of magazines, a little bar (open evenings) and elegant green drapes at the windows.

There are equally high standards in the bedrooms, which have hairdryers and tea/coffee makers. Women guests will find flowers in their bedrooms on arrival and there are even real wooden lavatory seats.

The dining room, with its attractive Welsh dresser, looks out onto a little patio hung with flower baskets. The English breakfast includes cheeses, hams, fresh melons and grapefruit as well as the usual bacon, eggs, etc.

The Kirkdale is situated on a quiet side street within easy reach of Croydon's shopping and business centre. A fax service is available for guests' use. Note that bathrooms have showers rather than bathtubs.

The prices are extremely reasonable: less than £50 for a double room with private bathroom during the week, and as low as £20 for a single at weekends. Very strongly recommended.

How to get there
British Rail from Victoria to East Croydon and then a short taxi ride. For drivers, the Kirkdale is within easy access of the A23 London/Gatwick Airprt/Brighton road.

Windsor Castle Toby Hotel

415 Brighton Road
South Croydon
Surrey CR2 6EJ
Tel 081 680 4559 Fax 081 680 5121

Price Band	£-£££ (much reduced weekend rates)
Credit Cards	All major credit cards
Bathrooms	Mainly private
Television	In rooms
Breakfast	English
Telephone	In rooms
Parking	45 parking spaces

It is always pleasant to discover a pub offering accommodation in the London area, as there are so few of them. The Windsor Castle is one of the country-wide Toby hotel group.

It is a handsome old whitwashed building standing on the Brighton Road, and is everything a good English pub should be: cosy, attractively decorated and friendly. Breakfasts, which include yogourt, kippers, fresh fruit, etc, as well as the usual bacon and eggs, are served in the bar, as are lunch and supper. A modern conservatory overlooks the garden, which is illuminated at night and where barbecue meals are served in the summer. There is even a bouncy castle for children at weekends.

The bedrooms are in a new wing to the rear of the pub. They are all very comfortable and equipped with tea/coffee makers, trouser presses and hairdryers. There is 24-hour room service, and a small function room for hire.

Prices tend to be negotiable and it is always worth asking for special discounts.

How to get there

British Rail from Victoria to Purley Oaks (every 15 min). Turn right out of the station and follow Brantwood Road until you see the hotel on the right. For drivers, it lies on the Brighton Road 2 miles south of the centre of Croydon.

Crystal Palace and Norwood

Crystal Palace Park is the former home of Joseph Paxton's magnificent glass palace which was originally erected in Hyde Park for the Great Exhibition of 1851, and subsequently dismantled and transported, piece by piece, and re-erected on this superb site in south London. Sadly, a fire in 1936 — the flames of which could be seen as far away as Brighton — destroyed all but its foundations and a few lonely urns and sphinxes.

However, the beautiful park, containing Victorian life-size models of prehistoric monsters, a little children's zoo and one of London's rare flocks of pink flamingoes, remains as a public open space.

Nowadays the park is home to the National Sports Centre and hosts a wide variety of sporting events, including swimming and athletics championships.

Although there are several hotels in the Crystal Palace area, they do not qualify for inclusion in this guide. Thus two hotels in Norwood, which is just a mile or so from the National Sports Centre, are recommended.

Norwood is a mainly residential area, developed in the latter part of the nineteenth century and famous only for its association with Sir Arthur Conan Doyle, who wrote a number of his Sherlock Holmes stories here at his home in Tennison Road.

Access to this area tends to be better by car than by public transport, the main route being the A23.

Places to Visit
Dulwich Park
Dulwich Picture Gallery
Horniman Museum

Norfolk Court Hotel

315 Beulah Hill
Upper Norwood
London SE19 3HW
Tel 081 670 3744
Fax 081 761 9246

Price Band	£-££ (reduced weekend rates)
Credit Cards	All major credit cards
Bathrooms	Mostly private
Television	In rooms
Breakfast	English
Telephone	In rooms
Parking	On hotel forecourt

The Norfolk Court was originally a large private house built as a wedding present in 1893. The original dark oak panelling has been retained in the unusually spacious reception area and an amusing poster on the wall proclaims: 'Visit Upper Norwood and Crystal Palace — The Fresh Air Suburb — 380 Feet Above the Thames and therefore out of the Valley Fogs'.

Although small (20 bedrooms), this hotel offers a full bar (evenings) and a suite for wedding receptions, conferences, etc. Its pretty terrace restaurant, with excellent views over South Croydon and the surrounding countryside is open to residents and non-residents for dinner.

The bedrooms have modern light wooden furniture, trouser presses and tea and coffee making facilities. The have been serviced for the last 17 years by the same chambermaid — a good indication of the high standards here. The staff are extremely helpful and friendly — the sort of place where guests feel immediately at home.

Ideally located for the National Sports Centre.

How to get there
British Rail from Victoria to West Norwood (every 20 minutes) then either bus 68 or 196 stop right outside the hotel, or a short taxi ride.

Norwood Lodge Hotel

17 South Norwood Hill
London SE25 6AA
Tel 081 653 3962
Fax 081 653 0332

Price Band	£-££
Credit Cards	Access/Visa/Delta/Mastercard
Bathrooms	Private
Television	In rooms and lounge
Breakfast	English
Telephone	In rooms
Parking	On hotel forecourt

Behind a nineteenth-century façade visitors to the Norfolk Lodge will find a modern interior furnished in the latest styles. The bedrooms have good quality pale wooden wardrobes and desks, attractive brass lamps, tea and coffee making facilities and trouser presses. They are bright and comfortable and exude a lovely smell of fresh soap. Those at the back overlook a large untended garden, where guests may relax on a summer's evening.

For relaxation, the hotel offers a spacious lounge with large comfy sofa, writing desk and piles of magazines.

Access to the dining room is via an unusual glass-roofed staircase. Like many of the bedrooms, it opens onto the garden and is therefore a pleasant place to start the day.

How to get there
British Rail from Victoria to Norwood Junction (frequent service). Turn right out of the station approach onto the main road and then left at the Albion public house. You will soon see the Norwood Lodge on the left. For those attending events at the Crystal Palace National Sports Centre, it is only one stop by British Rail train from Norwood Junction to Crystal Palace.

Ealing

A large borough, mainly residential, Ealing is situated west of the city centre, some thirty minutes by tube. A suburb with few outstanding features, its focus is the new shopping mall and it is, indeed an excellent shopping centre with branches of many of the main London stores in the Broadway and surrounding streets.

There are plenty of open green spaces; five minutes' walk from the Broadway is the delightful Walpole Park with a fine house, Pitshanger Manor, on its edge.

There is a good choice of restaurants, wine-bars and pubs. Ealing is well served by public transport. On the underground both District and Circle lines terminate here, British Rail runs regular services to Windsor and other interesting places to the west and it is a pleasant ride on the number 65 bus to Richmond.

Parking is very easy, so Ealing is a good location for visitors with cars.

Places to Visit

Kew Bridge Steam Museum   The Musical Museum
Kew Gardens   Pitshanger Manor Museum

Wellmeadow Lodge   £5 voucher scheme

24 Wellmeadow Road
London W7 2AL
Tel 081 567 7294
Fax 081 566 3468

Price Band	££
Credit Cards	All
Bathrooms	Private
Television	In rooms
Breakfast	English style
Telephones	In rooms
Parking	Plenty

Wellmeadow Lodge is a delightful little establishment which, while offering all the comforts of a hotel, is in many ways like staying in a home.

The well-lit hallway leads to a cosy sitting room, complete with an open fire, lots of books and plants and a welcoming drinks tray, and, also to the wonderful kitchen/dining room, full of dried flowers and herbs, where breakfast is taken at a huge farmhouse-type table. The meal itself is outstanding; all the usual cooked things being supplemented with home-made bread and preserves and real, freshly-squeezed orange juice.

A softly carpeted stairway leads to the bedrooms which are beautiful, full of sunny colours and well chosen antiques as well as extremely comfortable; Queen-size beds have orthopaedic mattresses, while tea/coffee makers, clock radios and even copies of the *Radio Times* complete the feel of luxury. Private bathrooms, added in 1993, have mahogany or pine vanity units with matching fitments, piles of fluffy towels, quality soaps and bathgels and even telephones!

Some of the double rooms have baths and separate power showers — something rarely seen outside a five-star hotel.

The Wellmeadow is faultlessly run by a young couple who really put themselves out for their guests, such as providing breakfast at any time between 7.30am and 11.30am, and obviously enjoy every moment of it. Highly recommended.

How to get there
Underground to Boston Manor, turn left out of station, take the first left and Wellmeadow is the first house on the left; about 2 minutes' walk in all.

Eltham

At first sight, Eltham, lying some 7 miles south-east of central London, is no more than an average suburb with its High Street shops and residential side streets. However, closer inspection reveals a large number of open spaces and two real treasures.

Tucked away at the end of a leafy lane, Eltham Palace consists of the Great Hall built by Edward IV in 1480 (this is all that remains of the original palace), a mansion house erected in the 1930s and a series of low, ruined walls, all surrounded by exquisite gardens and a moat.

Avery Hill Winter Garden, now part of a teachers' training college, is a massive Victorian glass dome housing all sorts of exotic plants and trees: breadfruit, date palms, bananas etc, overlooking gardens and extensive playing fields. Other open spaces include the Tarn (a public park and bird sanctuary), Well Hall Park (opposite Eltham station) and the Royal Blackheath Golf Course.

The great advantage of staying in Eltham is that it is only a couple of miles away from Greenwich, one of the most beautiful and most historic parts of London. In fact one could spend a delightful two or three days' break in this area without once going into central London, since there is so much to see and do here.

Bus No 286 runs from Eltham via Blackheath to Greenwich. British Rail trains run from Charing Cross to both Eltham and New Eltham every half hour. The A2 and A20 roads from the Channel ports pass through Eltham and parking is easy, making it very convenient.

Places to Visit

Cutty Sark	Avery Hill Winter Garden
Eltham Palace	Greenwich Park
Old Royal Observatory	Royal Naval College
National Maritime Museum	Thames Barrier

Yardley Court
18 Court Yard
Eltham
London SE9 5PZ
Tel 081 850 1850

Price Band	££
Credit Cards	Access, Visa
Bathrooms	Private and shared
Television	In rooms
Breakfast	English
Telephone	Public
Parking	Private car park

An old brick house painted in blue and covered in ivy and Virginia creeper, Yardley Court gives one the feeling of being in the country although Eltham is quite a busy suburb.

It has only nine bedrooms, all very prettily decorated, some with a little arch over the bed, others tucked in the attic under a skylight. They all have hairdryers and tea- and coffee-making facilities.

The dining room, which rises a few feet above the garden, is in the style of a conservatory, its long walls of glass allowing a maximum of sun and light to enter this lovely room. It is furnished with thick green carpet and a cane sofa and chairs. The Yardley Court has an excellent reputation for its breakfasts.

Strongly recommended.

How to get there
British Rail from Charing Cross to Eltham. Turn left out of the station, walk along Well Hall Road, cross over traffic lights at junction of Eltham High Street and the Yardley Court is on your right (5 minutes' walk).

Finsbury Park

Finsbury Park lies a little to the north of the centre, a journey of approximately 20 minutes by underground from Oxford Circus.

The Park itself is the area's most attractive feature and is at its best on a fine autumn day when the gold and russet leaves shimmer in the sunlight and the lake seems like a looking glass.

The famous Arsenal Football Club is within a 15 minute walk of Finsbury Park Station, and the area can be somewhat rowdy at match times and on Saturday nights. That said, the little shops along the main Blackstone Road have a friendly, well-established feel about them — especially the Italian delicatessens and the old-fashioned ironmongers.

For entertainment there are a number of pubs offering live music and in nearby Islington there is a wide range of theatre pubs, some of which include dinner with the show.

Although there are some fifteen or so hotels in Finsbury Park, mostly along Seven Sisters Road, overlooking the Park, currently only one meets our standards.

Places to Visit

Alexandra Park and Palace   Highgate Cemetery
Arsenal Football Club   Kings Head Pub Theatre
Haringay Stadium

New Pembury Hotel
328 Seven Sisters Road
Finsbury Park
London N4 2AP
Tel 081 800 5310
Fax 081 809 6362

Price Band	£-££ (reduced weekends & weekly rates)
Credit Cards	All major credit cards
Bathrooms	Private
Television	In rooms, plus Sky
Breakfast	English
Telephones	In rooms
Parking	Private car park, electronically controlled from reception.

'The Hottest Place in Hell' is how the new Pembury Hotel describes its spanking new 'fifties-style dining room. Open to both residents and non-residents for breakfast, lunch and dinner, it is a large, bright, fun room. It has striking red, yellow and blue tables and chairs, 'fifties adverts for Bristol Cigarettes and Raleigh Bicycles; pop music plays in the background, the bar is open in the evenings and a main meal can be had for under £5.

A sleek black 'fifties MG stands on the hotel forecourt, surrounded by flower tubs, wooden seats and benches so that diners can eat out on summer evenings.

The reception is marble-fronted and guests congregate there on sofas and easy chairs around a heart-shaped black coffee table. A lift whisks them up to the bedrooms — all recently refurbished and equipped with tea and coffee making facilities. Bathrooms are tiled in grey marble and prices are very negotiable.

Especially recommended to young people, and to those who have fond memories of the Buddy Holly era.

How to get there
Underground to Finsbury Park. Walk past the Finsbury Park Tavern and up Seven Sisters Road, with the Park on your left. The New Pembury is soon seen on the right.

Fulham

Fulham lies west of Chelsea on a bend of the River Thames. Though less fashionable than its famous neighbour, and often referred to as 'West Chelsea', it is a pleasant area, mainly residential, with some charming small streets leading off the New Kings Road. It is an antique hunter's paradise, with two auction rooms in Lots Road (auctions Monday and Thursday evenings) and almost every other shop selling antiques or collectables. Also here is Christopher Wray's Lighting Emporium, a stunning collection of light shades and fittings, many with Art Deco or Art Nouveau influences.

Among places of note along the river is the Hurlingham Club, popular for fashionable wedding receptions, and Fulham Palace, part of which dates from the early sixteenth century, now open to the public. The surrounding Bishops Park, is also open and a good place to watch the start of the famous Oxford and Cambridge Boat Race which takes place each year around Easter time.

Restaurants are plentiful in Fulham and many are reasonably priced, reflecting the pockets of the younger residents of this area. For summer dining those around Parsons Green have open-air terraces.

For transport three underground stations — Fulham Broadway, Parsons Green and Putney Bridge — serve the area and buses are plentiful.

Places to Visit
Bishop's Park and Fulham Palace

Pippa Pop-ins
430 Fulham Road
London SW6 IDU
Tel 071 385 2458 Fax 071 385 5706

Price Band	£
Credit Cards	All major credit cards
Bathrooms	Shared
Television	No
Breakfast	All home-made top quality children's fare
Telephone	Baby alarm intercom
Parking	Difficult

Pippa Pop-ins is London's only hotel exclusively for children, a fun alternative to employing a babysitter. The 'hotel' is also a nursery, so not surprisingly, it describes the accommodation as the 'Overnight Nursery'.

The Overnight Nursery has five large bedrooms and can take up to to twelve children between two and twelve years old. To quote from their brochure:

> Children are able to arrive in the late afternoon or early evening, and will be given a home-cooked and freshly prepared supper, before looking for the fairies that live in the garden. Magic bubble baths in the duck and clown bathrooms become enormous fun, and the bedtime stories that follow go on and on. All our nannies are qualified, have enormous experience, and are exceptionally good with children. Each of them has been very carefully recruited because of their genuine love of children and for their very warm, happy and fun natures.

Pippa's is indeed a Wonderland. Our visit was at Halloween, when a really wicked-looking witch was over-seeing a fearsome bubbling cauldron! Downstairs there is a little cloakroom containing three miniature lavatories, separated from each other by beautifully painted wooden Easter bunnies all flying red balloons.

Pippa's has been presented with the Consumer Association Hotel of the Year Award. Children should beg their parents to let them stay there.

How to get there
Underground to Fulham Broadway. Turn left out of the station and walk along Fulham Road for about 5 minutes until Pippa Pop-ins is seen on the left.

Greenwich and Blackheath

Greenwich is one of England's most beautiful and most historic sites. Greenwich Park, lying on a steep hill is one of the finest of London's Royal Parks. Here is the Old Royal Observatory, the Queen's House and the Royal Naval College with exquisite work by Inigo Jones, Wren, Hawksmoor and Vanbrugh.

Henry VIII and Elizabeth I were born here, and in 1806 Nelson's body was carried in state from the Painted Hall to St Paul's Cathedral. England's position as a great seafaring nation is displayed in the National Maritime Museum and by the presence of the sailing clipper *Cutty Sark* and Sir Francis Chichester's tiny sailing ketch, *Gipsy Moth IV*, in which he sailed around the world alone in 1966-7. Pleasure boats depart from Greenwich Pier to the Tower of London, Charing Cross and Westminster.

There are many good restaurants and tea shops in the centre of Greenwich and interesting pubs along the riverside, including The Trafalgar Tavern, immortalised by Dickens in his novel *Our Mutual Friend*.

Although less famous than Greenwich, Blackheath is also an attractive district. It has exclusive shops, residential streets, open heathland and fine architecture such as the Paragon and the seventeenth-century Morden College almshouses. It has good pubs, restaurants and an unusual tea shop in its Reminiscence Centre.

Despite its great beauty, this area is desperately short of hotels, let alone hotels of any character and only one here meets our standards. For that reason an excellent bed and breakfast is also included.

Places to Visit

Cutty Sark	National Maritime Museum
Fan Museum	Old Royal Observatory
Gipsy Moth IV	Ranger's House
Greenwich Park	Royal Naval College

Bardon Lodge Hotel   £5 voucher scheme

Stratheden Road
Blackheath, London SE3 7TH
Tel 081 853 4051   Fax 081 858 7387

Price Band	££-£££
Credit Cards	All major credit cards
Bathrooms	Mostly private
Television	In rooms
Breakfast	Continental
Telephone	In rooms
Parking	Plenty of private parking

Built in 1869, the same year as the *Cutty Sark*, Bardon Lodge has retained its original grandeur. The ground floor consists of spacious, high-ceilinged rooms with large marble fireplaces, a grandfather clock, prints of old London and luxurious curtains.

The Lamplight Restaurant is beautifully decorated in soft peach and burnt amber tones. An exciting menu uses exclusively fresh food; a three-course dinner averages about £16 while a set menu is around £10. The restaurant is open to residents and non-residents in the evenings Monday-Saturday and lunchtime Sunday.

The bar overlooks a well-tended garden and leads out onto a little patio where guests can relax in the summer.

The hotel also has several function rooms, ideal for wedding receptions, private parties and conferences. Laundry and secretarial services are available.

The bedrooms are as comfortable as the reception rooms, with tea and coffee making facilities.

Bardon Lodge has a superb location, just 15 minutes from London's M25 orbital motorway and 5 minutes' walk from Greenwich Park.

If coming on holiday to London the Bardon Lodge is close to many of the city's main attractions without having to struggle with the hustle and bustle of the centre. Very strongly recommended. Prices are negotiable, especially at weekends, so ask for reductions.

How to get there
British Rail train from Charing Cross to Blackheath, from which it is a short taxi ride. For drivers Bardon Lodge lies just off the heath and the main A2 Dover to London road, Shooters Hill.

Mr & Mrs C. Courtney

4 Egerton Drive
Greenwich, London SE10 8JR
Tel 081 691 5587

Price Band	£
Credit Cards	None
Bathrooms	Shared (showers in single rooms)
Television	In rooms
Breakfast	Continental
Telephone	Public
Parking	Parking vouchers at £1.50 per day

This pretty little B & B with just five bedrooms lies on a quiet side street close to Greenwich Station and dates from the 1820s. It has been completely restored and has all the modern conveniences, as well as both modern and antique furniture and a luxurious carpeted bathroom.

Downstairs is a cosy little dining room full of family mementoes. Guests are always welcome to pop in for a cup of tea or coffee and a chat at any time of the day. It is the sort of place that really feels like home.

Continental breakfast includes yogourt, fresh pineapple, peaches, as well as cereals, croissants and toast.

Prices are exceptionally low — £18 per person. Guests are requested not to smoke. Strongly recommended.

How to get there
British Rail from Charing Cross to Greenwich. Turn right out of the station and after a few minutes' walk Egerton Drive is on the left. Mr and Mrs Courtney's is towards the end on the right.

Hampstead

Lying to the north of the capital, Hampstead is one of the most beautiful of London's collection of 'villages'. The village first became fashionable in the eighteenth century due to the presence of medicinal springs. Clustered on and around its steep hills, Hampstead's houses are a true delight — seventeenth-century cottages with pretty little gardens, more formal eighteenth-century terraces such as those in Church Row, stately Victorian homes, and even a scattering of white weatherboard houses.

As well as its charming houses, Hampstead has a good selection of equally delightful pubs, restaurants, shops and continental-style cafés. There is even a little cinema, the Everyman, which in the 1920s was London's most exciting experimental theatre.

Any number of famous people have lived here over the years: the great actress Sarah Siddons had a house overlooking the Heath and the artist John Constable painted *The Romantic House in Hampstead* here and is himself buried in the churchyard in Church Row. South End was the scene of the last years of the tragic life of Hampstead's most famous poet, John Keats, who wrote his finest poetry here (in a house now named after him and open to the public) and at the age of only 26 died of consumption. Another house which is open to the public is Fenton House which dates from the late seventeenth century and which contains collections of early keyboard instruments, porcelain and exquisite furniture.

Beside the village lies the glorious Heath, 825 acres of park and woodland, beloved of walkers, picknickers, children, dogs and those just wishing to escape from the city centre to breathe fresh air. At the top of the hill stands Kenwood House, a fine eighteenth-century mansion, furnished in the style of the period and containing magnificent paintings by Gainsborough and Reynolds, two of that century's foremost artists. In the grounds of

Kenwood House, beside the lake, concerts of classical music are held on Saturday evenings during the summer.

At Bank Holiday weekends fairs are held at the southern end of the Heath and it also offers some of the best swimming in the London area — three beautiful, secluded ponds (mixed and single sex) surrounded by trees, complete with lifeguard and diving boards, and to which no admission fee whatsoever is charged.

Hampstead's underground station lies in the heart of the village and it is only 10 minutes by tube to the centre of London, making it one of the most attractive places for visitors to stay in the whole of the capital.

Places to visit
Burgh House
Fenton House
Freud Museum
Highgate Cemetery
Keat's House
Kenwood House
Waterlow Park

Hampstead Village Guesthouse

2 Kemplay Road   **£5 voucher scheme**
Hampstead
London NW3 1SY
Tel 071 435 8679
Fax 071 794 0254

Price Band	£-££
Credit Cards	All
Bathrooms	Private and shared
Television	In rooms
Breakfast	Optional extra (£5)
Telephone	In rooms
Parking	On street

It is difficult to do justice to the Hampstead Vill.
Guesthouse. It is certainly one of the very best sm.
hotels in its price range in London. Its charm lies not onl_
in the fact that the double-fronted Victorian house itself
is exquisite and retains many original features, but in the
fact that the rooms are crammed full of personal belong-
ings: books, records, a wickerwork basket etc, and that
two cats and two dogs are integral parts of the household.

In the dining room is a huge pine dresser, again
crammed with cups, plates, etc and to its left an old-
fashioned marble-topped sideboard. As they take breakfast, guests look out over pots of red geraniums standing
on a garden table. Whenever the weather permits breakfast is served in the garden itself.

The bedrooms, which include two interconnecting
rooms designed for families, are large and differ in style
from one to the other. Some have natural pine floors and
antique furniture.

Particularly attractive is the 'Blue' room which really
needs to be seen to be appreciated. All rooms have tea and
coffee making facilities, hairdryers and fridges. Many
also have trouser presses.

Popular with tourists, the hotel also serves business
people who need direct dial telephones, access to fax
facilities and to be able to entertain — Hampstead's
excellent restaurants are just around the corner.

Very, very good value for money. Strongly recommended.

Note that this is a non-smoking establishment.

How to get there
Underground to Hampstead. On leaving the station walk
down Hampstead High Street and turn left after some
five minutes into Pilgrim's Lane. Kemplay Road is then
the first street on the left and the Hampstead Village
Guest House is the first house on the right.

La Gaffe

107 Heath Street
Hampstead
London NW3 6SS
Tel 071 435 8965/8966
Fax 071 794 7592

Price Band	££
Credit Cards	Access/Amex/ Diners/Visa
Bathrooms	Private
Television	In rooms
Breakfast	Continental
Telephone	In rooms
Parking	Difficult

£5 voucher scheme

Definitely a place of character. One of a row of houses built in 1730, La Gaffe consists, on the ground floor, of a typical Italian restaurant and a lively café/bar. From there a staircase leads past a flower-decked roof terrace to the charming little bedrooms. Each one is named after an artist with prints of his work adorning the walls, or a theme such as the Campari Room. An adjacent cottage accommodates up to six people for longer stays.

Mr Bernado speaks four languages and, as he says, 'loves people'. Visitors come back time and again, as much for the atmosphere as for the area. He is constantly making improvements to his hotel: new, expensively tiled bathrooms and three pretty little honeymoon suites have recently been added. The uppermost of these has a four-poster bed with pink and blue drapes, a jacuzzi, an ingenious steam shower and lovely views over the roof and terrace garden. A super little hotel in a super area.

How to get there
Underground to Hampstead. Turn right out of the station and walk up the hill. La Gaffe is on the left.

The Langorf Hotel

£5 voucher scheme

20 Frognal
London NW3 6AG
Tel 071 794 4483 Toll free 1 800 925 4731
Fax 071 435 9055

Price Band	£££
Credit Cards	All
Bathrooms	Private
Television	In rooms, including satellite
Breakfast	Buffet
Telephone	In rooms
Parking	Pay and display

Set in a pleasant road of Victorian houses the Landorf Hotel is a new and attractive inclusion to this guide.

A short flight of smart terrazzo steps leads to a pleasant spacious reception area, papered in fresh blue and white stripes and with deep leather sofas. The bar/dining room has large windows overlooking the garden and serves a delicious breakfast of hams, cheeses and fresh-baked croissants. Light snacks and drinks are available at any time, while for other meals the hotel has an arrangement with several excellent local restaurants.

Bedrooms are really spacious, with seating areas, hospitality trays, hairdryers and super bathrooms.

The Langorf offers a wide range of facilities including a lift, 24-hour room service, and apartments for longer stay visitors. A friendly, personal yet professional service is combined with a superb location, within walking distance of the charms of Hampstead, yet quicker into the West End than many hotels within the central area.

Note that special rates are offered to readers of this guide, so mention this at the time of booking.

How to get there

Underground to Finchley Road. Turn left out of the station, crossing the busy Finchley Road. About three minutes' walk brings you to Frognal and the hotel is just around the corner on the right.

Hampton Wick and Kingston

Hampton Wick and Kingston face each other across a pretty stretch of the River Thames and are totally contrasting in styles. While Hampton retains its 'village' atmosphere, with rose-covered cottages and little shops, Kingston is a thriving shopping and business centre with a large number of modern buildings and a one-way traffic system. However, away from the traffic it boasts some pleasant riverside walks and a pier from which boats leave constantly, in summer, for many places of interest.

Kingston's chief claim to historical fame is the Coronation Stone, used to crown seven Saxon kings, which is preserved here.

Sports enthusiasts are well catered for with golf courses at Richmond, racing at Kempton and Sandown and tennis at Wimbledon all within easy reach.

Restaurants, wine-bars and pubs are, naturally, plentiful.

Although there is no underground at either Hampton or Kingston, central London is just twenty minutes away by train and bus services which are excellent.

Places to Visit
Bushey Park

Chessington World of Adventure (summer only)

Hampton Court Palace and Park

Kingston Heritage Centre

Richmond

Wimbledon Lawn Tennis Museum

Chase Lodge
10 Park Road
Hampton Wick
Kingston-upon-Thames
Surrey KTI 4AS
Tel 081 943 1862

Price Band	££
Credit Cards	Access/Amex/Visa
Bathrooms	Private
Television	In rooms
Breakfast	English
Telephone	In rooms
Parking	Plenty

£5 voucher scheme

This wonderful little hotel, built in 1870, won a well deserved award from the British Tourist Authority in 1992 as the best of its kind in England. Public areas are delightful, with warm colours, paintings and quality rugs. The newly enlarged bar/dining room, built on two levels, has an enormous bay window framed by ruffled curtains and a colour scheme of rich blue and apricot, complementing perfectly the antique pine furniture.

It would be hard to pick a favourite out of the ten individually designed bedrooms: some are in Laura Ashley style, others much bolder, like the Red Room with its fabric swathed walls and ceiling or the Honeymoon Suite with its four-poster bed. All, however, have clock-radios and tea/coffee makers. They, also, have quite the most enchanting bathrooms we have seen — pretty wallpaper, brass taps, little prints and antique pine making a welcome change from the usual stereotyped, albeit practical, tiles and marble.

The couple who own and run Chase Lodge do so with great charm and enthusiasm and win top marks for lovely little touches such as chocolates on your pillow every night, while still managing to keep room rates so competitive. Highly recommended.

How to get there
British Rail to Hampton Wick. Turn left out of station, right into Park Road, and you will see Chase Lodge on your right. Several bus routes pass the end of the road.

Pembroke Lodge

35 Cranes Park
Surbiton, Surrey KT5 8AB
Tel 081 390 0731

Price Band	£
Credit Cards	None
Bathrooms	Mainly shared
Television	In rooms
Breakfast	English
Telephone	Public
Parking	Plenty

What a delight, when exploring the residential roads of Surbiton, to come on this lovely little hotel: one of those rare places which wins top marks on all counts, its welcome and charm matching its value for money.

Spacious, comfortable bedrooms have attractive touches such as cushions strewn on the beds matching the curtains. All have tea/coffee makers and fridges, while those at the back have views over the beautiful garden and, in the distance, Hampton Court Palace.

However the outstanding feature of Pembroke Lodge is its elegant breakfast room which is worthy of a three-star hotel. Unusually situated on the first floor, pale green cloths cover the circular tables and a fine mahogany dresser supports a display of silver and crystal.

For disabled visitors a ground floor room has easy wheelchair access and breakfast can be served on a tray.

The over-riding impression at Pembroke Lodge, is of the wonderful welcome one receives.

How to get there
British Rail to Surbiton (just 15 minutes from Waterloo, frequent trains). Turn right up St Mark's Hill and, after the main crossroads of Surbiton Hill Road, Cranes Park is the first left. Bus 71, linking Surbiton with Kingston and Richmond, passes very nearby.

Harrow

Churchill and Byron, suburbia and commuters — this is Harrow, a definite two-part town. Above the grassy, wooded banks of its famous hill rises the majestic spire of St Mary's Church, a landmark for miles around, and close by nestle the buildings of one of the most famous public schools in the world — Harrow School, which numbers among its former pupils not only Churchill and Byron but a whole string of famous prime ministers, archbishops, kings and literary figures. Back on the 'mainland' it is a different story...!

Here you will find thousands of the semi-detached houses in their neat little gardens which typify true suburbia. These houses owe their existence to the expansion, between the wars, of the Metropolitan Railway, and they are largely occupied by families, the father taking this line to work every day in the West End or City.

Harrow-on-the-Hill has grown enormously over the last few years, and now has branches of many West End stores and an adequate supply of eating places.

Central London is approximately twenty minutes by tube and Wembley just ten minutes.

Places to Visit
Harrow School (by prior appointment)
Headstone Manor
St Mary's Church
Wembley Market (Sundays)
Wembley Stadium

Lindal Hotel

2 Hindes Road
Harrow
Middlesex HAI 1SJ
Tel 081 863 3164
Fax 081 427 5435

Price Band	££
Credit Cards	Access/Visa
Bathrooms	Mainly private
Television	In rooms
Breakfast	English style
Telephone	In rooms
Parking	Easy — large car park

Lindal Hotel has been owned and run by the same family for many years, during which time they have constantly improved it.

Mr Plunket, a former builder, maintains it perfectly, his wife puts the artistic touches, his son mans the reception while his daughter, who has worked in some of the five-star hotels in Mayfair, is the chef.

This family atmosphere, more often to be found in the countryside than in London, makes guests feel very much at home, especially business people, who have the added advantage of Fax facilities and writing space in their bedrooms, which also contain tea/coffee makers. Some rooms are non-smoking.

Unusually for a small hotel of twenty rooms the lounge-bar, where the local mayor was contentedly sipping a drink when I visited, and the restaurant are air-conditioned.

How to get there

Underground to Harrow-on-the-Hill. Turn right then first left up Station Road. On turning left into Hindes Road the hotel is immediately on your left, about ten minutes' walk in all. Taxis are available at the station.

Highgate

Highgate, like Hampstead, standing on a hill to the north of the city, is perhaps the most 'villagey' of London's villages.

The centre with its pond and arcaded shops, some of which date back to Georgian times retain charm akin to, yet quite different from, its more sophistocated neighbour. Of the many pubs the most famous is the Flask, an ancient coaching inn said to have been a haunt of the highwayman Dick Turpin, and equally delightful in summer or winter.

There are a few eating places in Highgate, while Hampsted with its abundance of cafés and restaurants is just five minutes away by bus or car.

Transport is by the Northern Line — about 15 minutes from the city centre.

Places to Visit
Alexandra Palace (venue for exhibitions and sporting events)
Kenwood House
Highgate Cemetery
Lauderdale House
Waterlow Park

Garden View Hotel

12 Shepherds Hill
London N6 5AQ
Tel 081 348 3376/7/8
Fax 081 348 5751

Price Band	££-£££
Credit Cards	All
Bathrooms	Private
Television	In rooms
Breakfast	English
Telephone	In rooms
Parking	Plenty on forecourt

'A country hotel in London' is a perfect description of this hotel which, while only a couple of minutes' walk from the underground, boasts a large and beautiful garden and is surrounded by woods and the glorious heath.

A pleasant reception area leads into the bar, which is furnished with leather sofas and has picture windows overlooking the garden and beyond. Drinks are served on the terrace in summer.

The restaurant serves good, medium-priced meals and traditional Sunday lunches, popular with locals.

Bedrooms, while not large, are pleasant and comfortable, all having hospitality trays and radios.

The Garden View Hotel is a relaxing place and the welcome from the manager and staff is warm and friendly

How to get there

Underground to Highgate. Take the exit through the carpark and you will see Shepherds Hill on your left. The hotel is a few steps down on the right.

Ilford and Forest Gate

Ilford and Forest Gate are largely residential areas lying some 6 or so miles north-east of the City. Clustered around Ilford station are all the shops one finds in a busy High Street, while Valentine's Park with its ornamental pond, bowling green and bandstand is only 10 minutes' walk away. A walk in the opposite direction will bring you to the much more open countryside of Wanstead Park.

All the hotels in this section are within a five-minute walk of a British Rail station and are therefore excellent choices for motorists and for people wishing to save money by staying a little outside the centre — a day pass for all four zones on the public transport system costs approximately £3.50.

The bus No 25 goes from Oxford Street via Holborn to Forest Gate and Ilford, but it is a fairly slow means of transport. For drivers, the M11 passes right through Ilford (particularly convenient for trips to Cambridge) and the M25 is only 8 miles distant.

There is little in the way of tourist attractions in this area: it is best to come into the centre, the journey time being approximately 30 minutes.

McCreadie Hotel

£5 voucher scheme

357-363 Romford Road
Forest Gate
London E7 8AA
Tel/Fax 081 555 8528

Price Band	£
Credit Cards	All major credit cards
Bathrooms	Private and shared
Television	In lounge and in rooms
Breakfast	English
Telephone	Public
Parking	Large private car park

Run by a friendly young English couple, the McCreadie Hotel is one of the very respectable small hotels to be found in that accommodation wasteland which stretches from Bloomsbury up to the borders of Essex. The hotel has seen various improvements over the last year, including the construction of a new bar (drinks available all day) and reception, and the opening of a games room.

Due to its location the McCreadie has a large business clientele, but it is also an excellent place for motorists (there is a large private car park) and for children. The hotel has a lovely big garden complete with goldfish pond, rabbit and swings.

The bedrooms are fairly simple, with some pretty quilts, the occasional easy chair, and tea and coffee making facilities. Note that there are no bathtubs, only showers. To qualify for the voucher discount visitors are requested to make bookings of two nights or more.

How to get there

Take the Central Line to Stratford, then British Rail to Forest Gate. Turn right out of the station and left into Romford Road at the traffic lights. The hotel is five minutes' walk. For drivers, the Romford Road is the A118 and the McCreadie is at the junction of Richmond Road.

Woodville Guest House

10 Argyle Road
Ilford
Essex IG1 2B0
Tel 081 478 3779

Price Band	£
Credit Cards	None
Bathrooms	Shared
Television	In rooms and in lounge
Breakfast	English
Telephone	Public
Parking	Private car park

The Woodville represents exceptional value for money —
for just £30 (1994) a night for a double room, guests may
enjoy the luxurious surroundings of an establishment
which would cost nearly twice the price in central London. The hotel is owned by a Scottish couple whose taste
is impeccable. On entering, one's gaze is immediately
drawn towards the delicate grey ceiling of the lounge
with its elegant chandelier, and towards the spacious
dining room beyond. Recently they have added a pretty
new reception area decorated with a vase of silk flowers.
A stag's head adorns the wall of the hall, bedrooms are
furnished with antiques and floral duvets and bathrooms
are carpeted — a real luxury in such a modestly priced
hotel. The bedrooms have tea and coffee making facilities. Note that the bathrooms have showers rather than
bathtubs.

A super hotel lying only five minutes' walk away from
the station — strongly recommended.

How to get there

Take the Central Line to Stratford and change onto
British Rail, alighting at Ilford. Turn left out of the
station and left into York Road. Argyle Road is the second
turning on the right and the Woodville is on the right.

York Hotel

£5 voucher scheme

8 York Road
Ilford, Essex IG1 3AD
Tel 081 514 1166
Fax 081 478 8107

Price Bank	£
Credit Cards	None
Bathrooms	Private and shared
Television	In rooms
Breakfast	English
Telephone	Public
Parking	Private car park

The York Hotel epitomises all that visitors to England expect to find in a good bed-and-breakfast hotel.

It is run by an English couple who really do put their heart and soul into making the guests feel at home: they will get up at the crack of dawn if you require early breakfast and they allow single girls to use a special bathroom which is out of bounds to males. They also tend the garden, look after the dogs and feed a baby fox which creeps along their hedge at dusk!

The bedrooms are very attractive (there is constant redecoration, although it would be hard ever to find any marks of wear and tear), but it is the dining room which is the *pièce de résistance*. Its walls are completely covered with a vast assortment of plates: modern, antique, humorous and delicate. Evening meals are available every night of the week which is very unusual for a hotel of this category in the London area. The bedrooms have tea and coffee making facilities and alarm radios.

An excellent little hotel, especially for motorists.

How to get there

Take the Central Line to Stratford and change onto British Rail, alighting at Ilford. Turn left out of the station and left into York Road. You will soon see the York Hotel on the right (three minutes' walk).

Kew and Richmond

Some half hour by tube west of the city centre by the River Thames, Kew and Richmond are two of London's most delightful 'villages'. Kew, is still little more than a village, with small shops and cafés surrounding the station, and pleasant tree-lined residential roads beyond.

In the world-renowned Botanical Gardens explore its 300 acres of woodland, lakes and flower plantations and, its majestic glasshouses. Anyone visiting London in May should not miss 'Bluebell time' at Kew — a carpet of purple beneath the tress stretching as far as the eye can see.

Richmond is more of a town, with a busy shopping centre and attractive antique and specialist shops in the smaller streets. It is also an area of open spaces; walk up Richmond Hill to Richmond Park, over two thousand acres of heathland and home to 600 freely roaming deer.

From Richmond Bridge, London's oldest (1777) there are delightful riverside walks in both directions.

Some of Richmond's most beautiful seventeenth- and eighteenth-century houses are situated around the Green, which is also overlooked by the charming Victorian terracotta-faced theatre. Restaurants, coffee shops, wine bars and pubs abound in Richmond — the standard, in general is high and prices reasonable.

Transport, too is excellent: Underground stations at Kew Gardens and Richmond (District Line) and British Rail at Richmond serve both central London and places to the west such as Windsor. Boat trips, in summer, to Westminster, Hampton Court, etc add to its attractions.

Places to Visit

Ham House	Orleans House
Kew Gardens	Richmond Park
Marble Hill House	Richmond Theatre

The Coach and Horses
8 The Green
Kew
Richmond
Surrey TW9 3BH
Tel 081 940 1208

Price Band	£
Credit Cards	Access/Visa
Bathrooms	Private showers (not WC)
Television	In rooms
Breakfast	English
Telephone	Payphone
Parking	Plenty

It is still fairly rare, in London, to find pubs which are also
hotels which is a pity because they offer a unique friendly
and lively atmosphere, as well as being much the most
reasonably priced accommodation where one can also get
a drink and a meal.

The Coach and Horses, however, is an exception:
picturesquely situated, right on Kew Green, it offers six
simple, spotless bedrooms above its bar and restaurant.
The pub area is cosy, as befits a former coaching inn,
parts of which date back to the sixteenth century, and the
menu on the blackboard, which changes daily, looks
quite delicious!

How to get there
Underground to Kew Gardens. Turn right, down Station
Avenue into Kew Gardens Road, turn left, then right at
the main road. The Coach and Horses is on the far side of
the green.

The Kew Gardens Hotel

292 Sandycombe Road
Kew
Surrey TW9 3NG
Tel 081 940 2220
Fax 081 332 6231

Price Band	££££
Credit cards	All
Bathrooms	Private
Television	In rooms
Breakfast	English style
Telephone	In rooms
Parking	Plenty

It is always a delight to come on a new hotel or, perhaps even more, to find one, previously run-down and depressing, which has changed hands and taken on a 'new lease of life' so spectacularly as the Kew Gardens Hotel.

This red-brick building, on approach, gives little clue to the loveliness of its interior, where, unusually for a hotel of only eighteen rooms there is a spacious bar and smart restaurant and reception area.

However, the *pièce de résistance* is the decor in the bedrooms; all are different yet with the same theme: shades of blues and yellows, beautifully expressed in Laura Ashley wallpapers, curtains and bedcovers.

Marble bathrooms are luxurious and filled with fluffy towels and quality toiletries.

The new owners of the Kew Gardens Hotel previously had a place in Winchester and have both enthusiasm and expertise; this is a lovely hotel which deserves to, and will, do very well.

How to get there

Underground to Kew Gardens. Come out onto Station Avenue and straight ahead into Sandycombe Road. The hotel is on the right.

The Plough

42 Christchurch Road
London SW14 7AF
Tel 081 876 7833

Price Band	££
Credit Cards	Access/Diners/Visa
Bathrooms	Private
Television	In rooms
Breakfast	English
Telephone	Payphone
Parking	Plenty

The Plough was built over two centuries ago and is the nearest thing you will find in London to a traditional country inn. The thick walls, black beams and the ancient plough hanging from the ceiling of the bar, makes you feel more in the country than the city. Of course, the fields which once surrounded it are now covered by houses but it is just a couple of minutes' walk to Richmond Park (the largest of the Royal Parks) where one can ride, play golf or just watch beautiful deer, descendants of those once hunted by Henry VIII, but now protected.

The Plough is surrounded by a pretty garden complete with hanging baskets and plenty of seating and the interior is cosy and welcoming. Cottage style bedrooms are decorated in light colours and all have tea/coffee making facilities. The delicious home cooking is recommended by Egon Ronay, and dinners as well as the usual lunchtime pub food are served.

How to get there

British Rail to Mortlake. Turn right into Sheen Lane and follow it as far as you can go, crossing the main Upper Richmond Road. At the end turn right into Christchurch Road and the Plough is on the corner. Richmond Underground station is about ten minutes by taxi (£3) and many buses pass nearby.

Riverside Hotel

23 Petersham Road
Richmond, Surrey TW10 6UH
Tel 081 940 1339
Fax 081 940 1339

Price Band	££
Credit Cards	Access/Amex, Visa
Bathrooms	Private
Television	In rooms
Breakfast	English
Telephone	In rooms
Parking	On street

From time to time one comes across a little hotel which fulfills all our criteria — pleasant location, comfortable rooms, good value and a friendly welcome; Riverside fulfills all of these. Set in a Victorian terrace, one immediately notices the snowy white drapes in the bay windows and brass carriage lamps flanking the front door.

Inside is cosy and welcoming: deep pile red carpet on the floor of the hall and stairway, bedrooms that are both comfortable and charming, some with river views and all with tea/coffee makers, and lovely bathrooms. The breakfast room and lounge are particularly attractive with windows both front and back (again views of the Thames), antique furniture and fresh flowers adorning the tables.

Riverside is deservedly popular with business people and holidaymakers so book well in advance to avoid disappointment, especially for rooms with a river view.

How to get there

Underground or train (British Rail) to Richmond. Turn left out of the station along the Quadrant, which becomes George Street. Bear left into Hill Street, which becomes Petersham Road after the bridge; Riverside is on the right. At least ten minutes' walk so those with luggage should take the 65 bus or a taxi. The romantic can always take a boat as the hotel is directly above Richmond Pier.

Maida Vale and Little Venice

Tucked between two long and unattractive thorough-fares, the Edgware and Harrow roads, Maida Vale is an oasis of peace; broad avenues of double-fronted, Victorian stucco houses are tree lined and although most of these houses, much too large for modern families, are now flats, they retain their elegance.

The focal point of the area is Little Venice, the junction of London's fifty miles of canalways and by far its most attractive spot, although those of you who have visited the real Venice may be a little disappointed! However, comparisons are odious and on a lovely spring or summer day this is a delightful place to be. At its widest spot Little Venice is spanned by two little bridges, painted blue and gold, and magnificent examples of the London Plane tree almost touch the water, while below artists paint, people relax on their brightly painted house boats and children feed the fluffy offspring of the geese, ducks and swans who make their homes here.

An added attraction is a floating restaurant and the colourful narrow boats, *Jason's Trip* and the *Jenny Wren*, which run regular trips to London Zoo and Camden Lock market.

There are several restaurants in the area and the West End is only ten minutes away by Underground (Warwick Avenue station on the District Line).

Places to Visit
Boat trips (summer only)
Lords Cricket Ground

The Colonnade

2 Warrington Crescent
London W9 1ER
Tel 071 286 1052
Fax 071 286 1057

Price Band	£££ - ££££
Credit Cards	Access/Amex/Visa
Bathrooms	Private
Television	In rooms
Breakfast	English
Telephone	In rooms
Parking	Free in street

The Colonnade, built in 1853 as two family houses, has since had a varied history: boarding school, nursing home, and from 1948 owned by the same family as a successful and popular hotel. This long-time ownership gives it an air of tradition not usually found in London hotels and has also meant it has never undergone a total refurbishment, as usually occurs when a hotel changes hands, but rather developed, bit by bit, over the years. Consequently just about every style of decor is to be found in the bedrooms, which vary from the quite ordinary to the supremely elegant suites which contain four-poster beds, jacuzzi baths, air-conditioning and teletext television. All, however, have hair-dryers and trouser-presses.

The most recent refurbishment was to the restaurant, now known as 'Cascades on the Crescent' where all meals are served to the relaxing accompaniment of an indoor waterfall. There is also an attractive cocktail bar, a lift and a pleasant garden with plenty of seating.

Definitely a place of character and tradition.

How to get there

Underground to Warwick Avenue. Turn right across Clifton Gardens and the hotel is right in front of you. Bus No 6 takes you to the West End in 10 minutes.

Wembley

Wembley first gained its international reputation in 1924 when it became the site for the British Empire Exhibition. Since then, and with the addition in 1934 of the Empire Pool (now known as the Wembley Arena), it has been an international sports and entertainments venue, hosting major events including the 1948 Olympic Games and the annual Football Association Cup Finals. In 1976 the Wembley Conference Centre, with a capacity of 2,700, was added to complete this enormous complex.

The 1924 Exhibition encouraged the growth of this area and most of its houses date from around that time. Wembley is a very typical 'Metroland' suburb of semi-detached houses, each with its own little garden.

Transport is very good with plenty of buses and a 15-minute journey time into central London on the Underground from Wembley Park Station.

Places to Visit
Harrow Heritage Centre
Wembley Stadium Tours

The Green Man
Dagmar Avenue
Wembley Hill Road
Wembley HA9 8DF
Tel 081 903 1441 Fax 081 902 6113

Price Band	££
Credit Cards	All major credit cards
Bathrooms	Private
Television	In rooms
Breakfast	English
Telephone	In rooms
Parking	Large private car park

The Green Man Hotel and Public House occupies a superb location on a little hill just above the Wembley Complex which is just 5 minutes' walk away. Only recently refurbished by an interior design company, it offers some of the best accommodation for miles around. The bedrooms have attractive dark varnished desks, chests of drawers and wardrobes. Matching these is a variety of quilted bedspreads, beautiful draped curtains and Laura Ashley style wallpapers. They all have tea and coffee-making facilities and irons, hairdryers and trouser presses are available on request. In the bathrooms, which are on the large size by London standards, guests will find a selection of complimentary toiletries. Bathrooms have both baths and showers.

Breakfast is served in the restaurant section of the bar. This is a really pretty little corner decorated with shelves of books, pots of dried flowers and prints of exotic butterflies. On the far side of the bar is a conservatory overlooking the garden. In the hot weather there are plenty of seats for guests on the lawn outside.

The bar and restaurant are open for the service of food and drink all day, from 11am to 11pm. A wide variety of dishes is available, ranging from roast dinners to cold buffets and traditional bar snacks.

The Green Man offers high quality accommodation combined with the informality and friendliness of a pub. Strongly recommended.

How to get there
Underground to Wembley Park and take a taxi which you will find right outside the station (approx £2).
Drivers: follow the signs for Wembley Complex. Dagmar Avenue is opposite The Wembley Conference Centre.

Wimbledon

Situated to the south-west of London, Wimbledon is one of the capital's more attractive suburbs. Mainly residential, the most prestigious area is around the park with its lake, horse riding and golf course; here the large detached houses standing in well manicured gardens make for many a pleasant stroll on a summer evening. Residents still refer to the centre as the 'village' which, these days, is something of a misnomer as it is busy, thriving and congested with traffic.

For most people, however, the name Wimbledon means just one thing, for it is synonymous the world over with lawn tennis and the famous championships that have been played here for over a hundred years. During those two weeks at the end of June/beginning of July this quite ordinary suburb takes on a touch of magic: perhaps the high spot of the London summer season, one meets few people who have not, at least once, enjoyed a lazy summer day here watching the play and eating delicious, though overpriced bowls of strawberries and cream. The atmosphere is tremendous and can never be captured on television. For the rest of the year one must be content with visiting the on-site museum with its attractive collection of tennis memorabilia. Among the area's other attractions are the Wimbledon Theatre, built in 1901, which stages pre-West End productions and the Polka Childrens' Theatre which is open from Tuesday to Saturday for plays, puppet shows and exhibitions.

Wimbledon has a good selection of restaurants, pubs and wine-bars and central London is just 35 minutes away by either Underground or British Rail. For motorists parking is easy and places of interest, such as Hampton Court and Windsor only a short drive away.

Places to Visit
Wimbledon Lawn Tennis Museum

The Wimbledon Hotel

78 Worple Road
London SW19 4HZ
Tel 081 946 9265
Fax 081 946 9265

Price Band	£
Credit Cards	Access, Diners, Visa
Bathrooms	Private
Television	In rooms
Breakfast	English
Telephone	In rooms
Parking	Plenty

A solid red-brick double fronted building, the Wimbledon Hotel is immediately warm and welcoming.

Decorated throughout in light colours with an attractive blue carpet, it has a pleasant ground-floor lounge and breakfast room and spacious, comfortable bedrooms, fitted with tea/coffee makers, clock-radios and lovely thick duvets on the beds.

Especially good for families as children are made very welcome and those under 8 years old stay free of charge.

Two ground-floor rooms are ideal for disabled visitors and wheelchair access is possible to one — a spacious double.

How to get there

Underground or train to Wimbledon, turn left into Wimbledon Hill Road. Worple Road is the second turning left and you will find the hotel on the left. Many buses pass the door.

AIRPORTS

Gatwick Airport and Horley

Gatwick, London's second airport, has grown enormously over the last few years and is no longer looked upon as the poor relation of Heathrow. Now taking scheduled as well as charter flights, it is quite likely that visitors to London will begin and end their trip here, and those whose flight timings dictate that they spend the first, or last, night locally are lucky as Horley, the little town nearby, has more than its share of good value small hotels. Taxis to and from the airport are plentiful and cost under £3, journey time is six or seven minutes.

Horley itself is unremarkable but it has an adequate selection of restaurants: an Indian, a Chinese and a pizzeria, while motorists can drive to one of the large airport hotels for a drink and a meal. However, those in search of something a bit special should take the ten-minute walk to Ye Olde Six Bells. Standing beside the River Mole, next to the twelfth-century St Bartholomew's church, this has been a pub for the last five hundred years, although its origins date back to AD857 when it was a retreat for the monks of Dorking Abbey.

Trains leave Victoria for Gatwick every 15 minutes from 6am to midnight and hourly through the night — journey time half-an-hour.

Stopping services stop at Horley but these are much slower, so the best advice is to use Gatwick station and take a taxi from there. There are also frequent trains to Brighton; locally known as 'London by the Sea' it is well worth visiting for its architecture and fine hotels, shops, restaurants and entertainments.

Chalet Guest House

77 Massetts Road
Horley, Surrey RH6 7EB
Tel 0293 821 666 Fax 0293 821 619

Price Band	£
Credit Cards	Access/Visa
Bathrooms	Private
Television	In rooms
Breakfast	Continental or English
Telephone	Public
Parking	Plenty

Totally refurbished, the Chalet is an excellent little hotel. Rooms are individual and most pleasing, mainly in the autumn colours the owner loves, even the net curtains match the general decor.

Guests may be sure of a friendly welcome, tea and coffee are available all day in the spotless kitchen and there is a small lounge for guests use. Parking is free and cars may be left for £10 per week during vacations.

How to get there
British Rail to Gatwick, then taxi. Alternatively train to Horley, walk down Victoria Road and Massetts Road is the second on the left. The Chalet is on the left-hand side.

The Cottage

33 Massetts Road
Horley, Surrey RH6 7DQ
Tel 0293 775 341 Fax 0293 783 812

Price Band	£
Credit Cards	Access/Visa
Bathrooms	Public
Television	In Rooms
Breakfast	Continental, served in rooms
Telephone	Public
Parking	Plenty

The Cottage is aptly named: a pretty black and white timbered house with roses round the door and a real country feel to it.

The five guest rooms have tea/coffee making facilities, television and radio-alarms for early departures. These, with their latch door handles, flower-sprigged bed linen and sloping ceilings fit in perfectly with the country cottage exterior.

The Cottage is run by a delightful, friendly young mother whose husband, an Italian, also speaks Spanish, so languages are well catered for here.

Parking is free and guests may also leave their cars here, during holidays, for £10 per week.

How to get there
British Rail to Gatwick, then taxi. Alternatively train to Horley, walk down Victoria Road and Massetts Road is the second on the left.

The Lawn Guest House

30 Massetts Road
Horley
Surrey RH6 7DI
Tel 0293 775751
Fax 0293 821803

Price Band	£
Credit Cards	Access/Visa
Bathrooms	Mainly private
Television	In rooms
Breakfast	English
Telephone	Payphone
Parking	Plenty

One is welcomed to the Lawn Guest House by the friendly owners and their two adorable golden labrador dogs.

Breakfast is served in the pleasant little dining room, a dresser at one end covered by the same pretty blue and white china which adorns the tables.

The bedrooms have large windows overlooking the pretty, well-kept garden and are spacious enough to hold armchairs and coffee tables as well as good sized beds covered by fresh, flowery duvets.

An excellent little hotel which has recently been further improved.

How to get there
From London British Rail to Gatwick, then taxi. Alternatively train to Horley, walk down Victoria Road and Massetts Road is the second on the left.

Rosemead Guest House
19 Church Road
Horley
Surrey RH6 7EY
Tel 0293 784965
Fax 0293 820438

Price Band	£
Credit cards	None
Bathrooms	Shared
Television	In rooms
Breakfast	English
Telephone	Payphone
Parking	Plenty

Another good little hotel in an area, unlike central London, where one is really spoilt for choice.

Working in close co-operation with the Lawn Guest House, Rosemead offers the same friendly welcome with hosts who always have time for, and enjoy talking to, their guests.

Public areas are pleasant and bedrooms spacious and absolutely spotless.

Children and dogs welcome.

How to get there

From London take British Rail to Gatwick, then taxi. For motorists Church Road is a turning off the main A23 near the Chequers Hotel.

Vulcan Lodge

27 Massetts Road
Horley
Surrey RH6 7DQ
Tel 0293 771 522

Price Band	£
Credit Cards	Access/Visa
Bathrooms	3 private, 1 public
Television	In rooms
Breakfast	English
Telephone	Public
Parking	Plenty

Like a four-star hotel in miniature, no expense has been spared to make Vulcan Lodge quite perfect. This tiny but enchanting house, consisting of only four rooms, has both comfort and charm in abundance. Decor is in Laura Ashley style with flower-sprigged wallpaper, frilled window blinds, soft lighting, original pine doors and floors to match, the latter strewn with quality rugs.

Everywhere small touches show the owners' good taste and enthusiasm — not surprising, therefore, that many guests, originally booking for just one night, end up spending their vacation here!

How to get there

British Rail to Gatwick, then taxi. Alternatively train to Horley, walk down Victoria Road and Massetts Road is the second on the left.

Heathrow

After many days spent searching around Heathrow Airport, we reluctantly came to the conclusion that none of the small hotels in this area met our standards.

For those travelling by underground the nearest is the delightful Wellmeadow Lodge (listed under Ealing), which is just 15 minutes' journey or, if this is fully booked, anywhere on the Piccadilly Line. Visitors with cars try Richmond — 10 minutes' drive.

Alternatively the large airport hotels often offer special rates, especially at weekends.

Children

For the first time, this edition includes a hotel which is exclusively for children — Pippa Pop-ins.

Among the other hotels in this guide the following are particularly welcoming to children

Camelot Hotel	Mitre House Hotel
Centaur Hotel	Parkwood Hotel
Edward Lear Hotel	Ridgemount Hotel
Garden Court	Rosemead Guest House
Lawn Guest House	Wimbledon Hotel
McCreadie Hotel	

Car Parking

At the following hotels car parking is possible. As might be expected parking is less of a problem in Outer London than in the city centre, so this might be an important factor when choosing where to stay.

Arran (limited)	Cecil Court (limited)
Bardon Lodge	Centaur
Blyth	Central
Broughton, Mr & Mrs	Chalet Guest House

Chase Lodge
Chiswick
Coach and Horses
Colonnade
Cottage, The
Europa House (limited)
Fairways (limited)
Garden View
Green Man
Grianan
Hampstead Village Guest-
    house (limited)
Kew Gardens
Kirkdale
Lawn Guest House
Lindal
McCreadie

Mitre House
New Pembury
Norfolk Court
Norwood Lodge
Plough, The
Queensway (limited)
Riverside
Rosemead Guest House
Vulcan Lodge
Wellmeadow Lodge
Wimbledon
Windmill on the Common
Windsor Castle
Woodville
Yardley Court
York

Disabled

The Holiday Care Service is a charity which advises disabled people on accommodation in London. You may contact them at:

2 Old Bank Chambers
Station Road
Horley
Surrey RH6 9HW
Tel 0293 774535

Since most of London's smaller hotels have not been purpose-built and are often more than 100 years old, they tend to be unsuitable for people with wheelchairs — the majority have a flight of six steps up to the front door and not all have lifts.

However the Wimbledon Hotel (page 149), the Pembroke Lodge at Kingston (page 130) and the Windmill on the common at Clapham (page 103) have ground floor rooms with easy wheelchair access.

Hotel Index